D0765177

UNFINISHED BUSINESS:
AN AGENDA FOR LABOR,
MANAGEMENT, AND THE PUBLIC

Proposed by Seven Secretaries of Labor

Arthur J. Goldberg
Willard Wirtz
George P. Shultz
James D. Hodgson
John T. Dunlop
William J. Usery, Jr.
F. Ray Marshall

UNFINISHED BUSINESS:
AN AGENDA FOR LABOR, MANAGEMENT, AND THE PUBLIC

Edited by
Abraham J. Siegel and David B. Lipsky

The MIT Press
Cambridge, Massachusetts, and London, England

This book was set in VIP Times Roman by Grafacon, Inc., printed
and bound by Murray Printing Company in the United States of
America

Library of Congress Cataloging in Publication Data
Main entry under title:

Unfinished business.

   1. Labor policy—United States—Addresses, essays, lectures.
2. Industrial relations—United States—Addresses, essays, lectures.
I. Siegel, Abraham J. II. Lipsky, David B., 1939–
HD8072.U53   331′.0973   78–16170
ISBN 0–262–19175–X

Contents

James D. Hodgson, John T. Dunlop, Arthur J. Goldberg, Willard Wirtz, William J. Usery, Jr.

Preface

When Ray Marshall became President Jimmy Carter's secretary of labor in January 1977, it marked the eighth time in sixteen years that a new secretary had taken charge of the Department of Labor. This record of high turnover in an important cabinet position, not unique to the Department of Labor, was perhaps symptomatic of the general tumult and instability in the nation in the 1960s and early 1970s. Few would deny that the period bracketed by the presidencies of John F. Kennedy and Jimmy Carter constituted an era of immense significance in American history. The civil rights revolution, an unpopular foreign war, and a major domestic political scandal were only three of many forces that strained the capacities of our constitutional government and its elected and appointed leaders. By 1976 an era of continuing crises seemed to have passed and a new era of reconstruction and reconciliation seemed to be possible. To be sure, the issues on the national agenda were and are no less difficult or intractable than those of the preceding sixteen years. But there was, at least, the hope that solutions for the nation's problems could be sought with far less din and disruption and far more reason and sober reflection than had often been possible in the recent past.

March 1977 thus appeared to be a particularly good time for stocktaking—a time to trace where we had been and to chart a course for the future. Certainly many of the most critical issues on the new administration's agenda were matters central to the Department of Labor's concerns. Some of these issues were of relatively recent origin, while others had, in one form or another, been on the nation's agenda for a long period and had been carried forward from president to president and from secretary to secretary. The moment seemed ripe to convene a meeting of the former secretaries to obtain their current assessment of the nature of the issues the new secretary faced, the priorities that ought to be attached to them, and some possible methods of achieving the nation's goals associated with the identified issues.

The institution of the presidency was, needless to say, severely tested during the 1960s and 1970s. This period of presidential assassination, resignation, and defeat at the polls had its impact on all cabinet positions, including that of secretary of labor. But throughout this trying period the nation was fortunate to have several exceptionally able persons serve as secretary. In the papers contained in this volume, two of these secretaries, Willard Wirtz and George Shultz, credit the firm establishment of the department's bipartisan professionalism largely to one of their predecessors, James Mitchell, who was secretary under President Eisenhower. But the secretaries who followed Mitchell surely sustained and enhanced the department's reputation for integrity and professionalism. Throughout the period the department was never affected by a major scandal.

Further, although it is the government agency charged with

maintaining an equitable balance between management and labor—never an easy task under the best of circumstances—the Labor Department has earned the respect of both unions and employers, not to mention academics and neutrals who specialize in labor relations.

The department's commitment to professionalism is essential to the fulfillment of its mission. It is charged with many sensitive tasks, including the enforcement of wage and hour legislation, the administration of billions of dollars of public employment and training funds, the regulation of thousands of pension plans, the achievement of safe and healthful working conditions in millions of workplaces, the collection of politically sensitive employment statistics. Such tasks are the stuff of controversy, and the department receives its share of criticism. But its commitment to professionalism, to the development and application of the specialized knowledge and expertise that is necessary to the fulfillment of its mission, is seldom questioned. The capable men and women who have served as secretaries of the department have all been professionals of the first rank.

Many of the most critical issues of the last decade and a half directly involved and tested the mettle of the secretary of the Department of Labor. Unemployment and inflation, job safety and health, strikes in major industries, income-maintenance programs, and many other issues were squarely in the secretary's domain. The secretary's responses to these problems—his ability to shape and administer appropriate policies, his relations with the president, his influence on the Congress, his dealings with the labor and management communities—all had a significant impact on the domestic welfare of the American people.

Able people occupied the position, but surely one of the costs of the instability of the recent past was that most were unable to serve long enough to see many of their policies through to implementation. Of the seven men who served as secretary of labor from 1961 to 1977 only one—Willard Wirtz—held office for more than three years. By contrast, over the department's first 48 years (1913–1961), it had only eight secretaries, and one, Frances Perkins, served for 12 years under Franklin D. Roosevelt. That kind of continuity was an advantage the Department of Labor was not afforded for most of the 1960s and 1970s. Yet over the more recent period the department's responsibilities have increased at an almost awesome rate. John Dunlop points out that the department had 16 major statutes to administer in 1940 and 134 in 1975, and most of the latter were passed in the 1960–1975 period. Further, when Arthur Goldberg became secretary, the department had 6,000 employees, but when Secretary Marshall took office, it had more than 14,000. The Labor Department may be small compared to the Departments of Defense and of Health, Education, and Welfare; still, few have grown more rapidly or taken on such important responsibilities in so brief a period of time.

All the secretaries represented in this volume were and continue to be acutely concerned about the increasingly complex managerial role of the secretary and the growing regulatory burden of the department. Most believe that the smaller size of the department in the past was a virtue that aided managerial effectiveness and efficiency. But they worry that growing complexity and bureaucratization will handicap the secretary and make the department less effective.

Their short tenure in office combined with an ever-increasing number of statutes and programs to administer clearly caused not merely concern but also frustration for several of the secretaries. Several had barely finished a period of on-the-job training when for various reasons they had to move on to a different assignment. In the period they were on the job, they generated an agenda based on their goals and priorities, but they generally lacked the time to complete many of the tasks they set. This conference provided them the joint opportunity to indicate to which agenda items they would now give a high priority and which new goals they believed the current secretary of labor might best pursue.

There is significant consensus in the secretaries' remarks on three broad topics. First, they all stress the urgency of the unemployment problem, particularly among minorities and young people. Second, they all express a strong belief in collective bargaining and believe it is working well in this country. Third, they are all concerned about the regulatory burden borne by the secretary and the department and its import for society.

There are differences among them, however, in their analysis of the root of the unemployment problem and in their proposed method for solving it. For example, Secretary Usery seems to feel that we *can* solve the unemployment problem, that we possess the technical know-how to do so but that we lack the commitment, the *will*, to do so. Secretary Dunlop, on the other hand, says, "We still do not understand how jobs are created in our society." He contends that "it is not simply a matter of our knowing what to do but lacking the will to do it. Rather, we have arrived at a stage where we do not really know what to do about the economy."

As for the methods they would choose, Secretary Wirtz stresses the importance of manpower policy, especially when linked to educational policy. But Secretary Hodgson's experience as ambassador to Japan makes him skeptical about the effectiveness of remedial manpower policies. He points out that the Japanese "have not undertaken extensive government manpower programs," but that they have "realized some fairly impressive manpower achievements." Hodgson would seem to agree with Wirtz, however, when he commends a basic education that equips the student with "full literacy" and a "usable, marketable skill."

Among other differences that might be noted, only Secretary Shultz explicitly places some of the blame for high unemployment among young people on "the high and undifferentiated minimum wage." And Secretary Goldberg stands alone in advocating the necessity of an incomes policy, that is, wage and price controls, to restrain inflationary pressures while the nation struggles to lower the unemployment rate.

On the subject of collective bargaining, the secretaries, and indeed both union and management participants, are nearly unanimous in believing that our system is working well. Secretary Wirtz refers to the "miracle of collective bargaining," a refrain that is subsequently picked up by several conference participants. Secretary Dunlop, in pursuing this theme, expresses the thought that it is "the duty of the secretary of labor to explain to the public the central importance of collective bargaining and free trade unions in modern society." While praising the collective-bargaining process and urging the secretary of labor to articulate its importance, the former secretaries suggest minimal changes in the current system. Secretary Wirtz recommends extension of the national labor law to cover agricultural and nonprofit employees and also supports repeal of Section 14(b)—the section of the law that allows states to ban the union shop. He further supports amendments to permit common situs picketing. Secretary Shultz counsels tolerance of strikes; he feels that the secretary of labor should minimize his intervention in labor negotiations. Secretary Goldberg, by contrast, advocates a more activist role for the secretary, an approach he put into practice while he served in that office.

The secretaries probably did not know in March 1977 that the new Carter administration would push strongly for labor-law reform, and therefore they are largely silent on this issue. Secretary Marshall, however, in remarks delivered at the conference by Undersecretary Robert Brown, did stress the need for labor-law reform. This theme is picked up most forcefully by the union representatives on the panel, particularly Stephen Schlossberg of the UAW and Thomas Donahue of the AFL-CIO. At the time of the conference, the issue of common situs picketing was still very much alive and was heatedly debated by the panel. For example, John Lyons, president of the Iron Workers, states the case for common situs picketing, while Dale Stone, senior vice-president of the Sun Company, argues strongly against it. Their arguments will no doubt be raised again if and when the common situs picketing bill is resurrected in the Congress.

The third theme sounded by almost all the secretaries concerns the heavy regulatory burden carried by the Department of Labor. Most seemed to agree with the view expressed by Secretary Dunlop: "I think we have reached the stage where the legal model, which involves the process of promulgating regulations, the subsequent litigious activities, and the game-playing between the regulators and the regulatees, has seriously interfered with the collective-bargaining process and the achievement of our social purposes." Concern about the problem of overregulation is expressed again and again, throughout the conference, by all participants. Secretary Marshall's remarks reflect the Carter administration's recognition of the problem of overregulation. Marshall promises: "The Occupational Safety and Health Act (OSHA) and the Employee Retirement Income Security Act (ERISA) will be major targets in our efforts to simplify complex government regulatory programs and relieve unnecessary administrative and paperwork burdens on employers." Within a few months of the conference (and while this volume was being prepared for publication), the administration had taken steps to begin to fulfill this promise by dropping over 1,100 OSHA regulations and otherwise simplifying OSHA's regulatory procedures.

But Secretary Dunlop and others seem to feel that the regulatory problem will not be a simple one to solve, since it is merely a symptom of deep-rooted tendencies in the American culture. If, in fact, the tendency to overregulation in the United States is culturally determined, it may be the most persistent of all the problems discussed at the conference.

In addition to these common concerns, each secretary has his own particular set of interests—reform of the unemployment insurance system (Wirtz), implementation of a negative income tax (Shultz), questions about participation in the International Labor Organization (Dunlop). Moreover, the discussants on the panel suggest additional concerns they feel need to be on Secretary Marshall's agenda. The topics mentioned by the conference participants are numerous and reflect the diversity of responsibilities falling within the Department of Labor's province.

Whether the incumbent secretary can or should attempt to tackle all the issues raised in this volume is problematic. Nevertheless, it is clear that instruction in the proper course of public policy has seldom been offered by a group of tutors so experienced or distinguished.

Acknowledgments

We are, of course, exceedingly grateful to the six former secretaries, the current secretary of the Department of Labor, and the panel of six union and management leaders who agreed to participate in this exchange of views. The conference audience of 200 union and management representatives, government officials, neutrals, and academic specialists in industrial relations helped sharpen the discussion, and we are pleased to acknowledge their contributions.

In addition, we would like to thank Charles A. Myers, director of the Industrial Relations Section at the Sloan School of Management, for his help in organizing the conference and Howard W. Johnson, chairman of the MIT Corporation, for his personal support and for the help provided us by Betty Whittaker and other members of his staff. We also owe much to W. William Suojanen, who helped make the conference run smoothly, and to Grace Locke, Susan Radley, Joyce Wright, Maxine Henry, and Missy Harrington, who assisted with the details of the conference and the typing of this manuscript. Finally, we were fortunate in securing financial support from the Henry Luce Foundation toward realizing our conception of a stimulating occasion. Our personal thanks go to Martha Wallace of that foundation for her steady encouragement and support.

REMARKS OF THE
SECRETARIES OF LABOR

Arthur J. Goldberg
(1961–1962)

Arthur J. Goldberg was the American labor movement's chief legal strategist before becoming one of the most active members of President Kennedy's cabinet. Born in 1908, he received his J. D. degree summa cum laude from Northwestern University, went on to specialize in labor law, and during World War II served with the Office of Strategic Services. In 1948 he was named general counsel for the United Steelworkers of America and the Congress of Industrial Organizations.

Goldberg played a major role in the merger of the CIO and the AFL and in the development of pension and insurance plans for workers. He was named secretary of labor in 1960 and served in the office through September 20, 1962, when he resigned after President Kennedy announced his appointment to the U.S. Supreme Court to succeed Felix Frankfurter.

Within 72 hours of being sworn in as secretary, Goldberg settled a disruptive New York tugboat strike. Later he helped negotiate maritime and airline strike settlements, won a no-strike pledge at missile construction sites, and mediated a dispute that had threatened to cancel the 1961–1962

Metropolitan Opera season. In 1962 he helped the parties reach a settlement in the steel and railroad industries.

Goldberg was sworn in as associate justice of the Supreme Court on October 1, 1962, and served there until July 1965 when he agreed to take the post of U.S. representative at the United Nations following the sudden death of Ambassador Adlai Stevenson. Goldberg was active in early efforts to secure peace in southeast Asia and, as president of the Security Council, played an important part in negotiations leading to the cease-fire between India and Pakistan. In 1968 he returned to a private law practice where he has continued to garner many honors.

In commencing this discussion, I should put you on notice that I no longer profess expertise in this area.

When I became secretary of labor, I advised the Senate Labor Committee on my own motion that in future private life I would not resume an active role representing labor in industrial disputes. And I have not assumed such a role since 1961. I made this statement because of my long opposition to the process whereby a regulator leaving government joins a private interest he or she formerly regulated. This process has contributed to the understandable yet regrettable cynicism of the public toward government and government officials.

My comments, therefore, are those of an emeritus expert, conscious that time works changes and that there have been many significant developments in collective bargaining in the past fifteen years. But you have solicited my views, and I shall state them for whatever value they may have in exploring the subject of the conference, in improving free collective bargaining, and in seeking to make our economy healthy and responsive to the needs of labor, management, and the public.

I continue to be a strong believer in free collective bargaining as the major means of wage determination in our industrial democracy. While favoring voluntary arbitration, I remain opposed to compulsory arbitration and, correspondingly, am against government-imposed settlement of collective-bargaining issues in both small industries and large. But I quickly add that whenever the national health, safety, or economy is significantly involved, it is my belief that any administration should act unhesitatingly to safeguard the nation with all the means Congress has provided and, if these are inadequate, recommend to Congress additional means.

It remains my conviction that in a free society employees and employers must be permitted to assert their economic force in collective-bargaining situations, except in cases of national emergency as just defined.

While recognizing the necessity for preserving this key aspect of collective bargaining, I believe it to be the responsibility of the parties and the government also to seek by all available means to minimize economic conflict in collective bargaining. Recourse to economic force should always be a last resort.

No administration can remain disinterested in the total result of collective bargaining in the country and whether it leads or contributes to a sound or an inflationary economy and to justice and fairness to all involved in the process and to the public as well.

Further, no government can be disinterested in whether particular bargaining leads to industrial peace or economic war in which the public interest may be severely injured.

The challenge of collective bargaining is to serve the respective constituencies of the parties and also to serve the public interest.

The key to meeting this challenge is in the interrelationship of freedom and responsibility. To be free, collective bargaining must be responsible; so long as collective bargaining is responsible, it will remain free.

"Free," of course, means free to exercise the right of final decision-making. It does not and cannot exclude government concern, interest, "good offices" procedures, and mediation—all of which are traditionally compatible with and helpful to freedom in this area.

"Responsible" means that collective bargaining must be responsive to the interests of the parties, the employers, and the workers, but responsible also to the common interest, the public interest.

And government, of course, must act responsibly, too. Collective bargaining does not operate in a vacuum. Collective bargaining alone cannot and does not determine the total economic result. Government policies determine the nation's economic health to a far greater degree than collective bargaining.

This is not to say that collective bargaining does not in some measure contribute to inflationary trends and affect the nation's economy. Certainly wage increases exceeding productivity are a factor. But workers simply cannot be expected to moderate their wage demands at the expense of their living standards while prices and profits remain unrestrained. And employers, in turn, cannot be expected to absorb increasing costs arising from collective bargaining without protecting reasonable profit margins.

President Carter has offered an economic program to Congress. It has been criticized from two directions. One set of critics, including the labor movement, has a twofold argument against it: first, it is not large enough to provide adequate economic stimulation of the economy, and second, it is misdirected in providing excessive tax relief rather than increasing the amount of money available for job creation. Critics on the other side argue that it will have inflationary effects outweighing the benefits that may accrue, that job creation by direct governmental expenditure is too slow and expensive, that the public interest would be better served by increasing tax incentives to business.

The president's proposals will be modified by Congress, and the complete economic package as proposed or modified has not yet been adopted. There are, however, some disturbing developments in anticipation of the proposed economic package. Interest rates and the consumer cost-of-living index have already begun to rise. These trends, unless reversed, obviously will mean more inflation.

I assume all will agree that unemployment and inflation are the two priority domestic economic problems facing the country. It is my view that if the government is to deal with unemployment on a scale commensurate with its extent and is in general to treat adequately with the current recession, a larger program in terms of both job creation and tax reduction is required. But it is also my belief that to avoid the inflationary consequences of such a program, the government will have to adopt an incomes policy.

What the nature of the incomes policy should be will depend upon and perhaps be determined by developments. A revival of the President's Labor-Management Committee is to be welcomed. A prior-notification policy may or may not be adequate. Standby authority to impose wage and price controls may prove to be necessary, and one cannot rule out the imposition of such controls.

In light of the allergy of labor and management to any incomes policy, however limited, it is the counsel of wisdom to proceed cautiously in this sensitive area. But not so cautiously that the horse is out of the barn before the door is closed.

I have no illusions about the political difficulties of fashioning and adopting an adequate incomes policy. It is, however, a fringe benefit of one who does not have the responsibility of office to raise the issue. I do so with the conviction that in the final analysis the interests involved and the general public will support whatever actions need be taken to cope with our economic ills.

Willard Wirtz
(1962–1969)

Willard Wirtz was born in 1912 in Dekalb, Illinois. He attended North Illinois State Teachers College and the University of California at Berkeley. He received his B.A. from Beloit College in 1933 and his J.D. from Harvard Law School in 1937. He was assistant professor of law at Northwestern University from 1939 to 1942, when he went to Washington to serve as assistant general counsel to the Board of Economic Welfare. From 1943 to 1945 he was with the War Labor Board and served as general counsel and public member on the board in 1945 and as chairman of the National Wage Stabilization Board in 1946.

He returned to Northwestern University Law School in 1946 as a professor. In 1954 he returned to private practice and served as arbitrator in a number of major labor-management disputes.

Wirtz was appointed undersecretary of labor in 1961, and in 1962 he succeeded Arthur Goldberg as secretary, an office he held through the Kennedy and Johnson administrations.

In 1969 he returned once again to private practice, but he has continued to serve in major roles as member or head of a number of commissions concerned with both labor relations and employment matters. One of these is the National Manpower Institute, of which he is currently president.

The task of describing my "unfinished agenda" as secretary of labor is simplified by the fact that I did just this in a speech delivered on my last day in office, back in 1969.

The speech is contained in the *Fifty-Sixth Annual Report of the United States Department of Labor*. All the labor secretaries are required by law, I think, to make them every year. In this annual report I said, "It would be easier to conclude from a review of the first fifty-five volumes in this series of annual reports that some one person had written them all than that any of the ten secretaries of labor, including the incumbent, had taken significant part in the preparation of even one of them." The *Fifty-Sixth Annual Report* then said, in a fairly self-serving fashion as I look back on it, that it was a waste of the taxpayer's time to read the earlier reports and therefore in my final report I would draw from the record whatever instruction it offered the future and would put special emphasis on those items that had more to say to the future than to the present.

The interesting thing is that the *Report* has hardly anything to say about the subjects to which Arthur Goldberg has spoken so directly. It seemed to me in 1968 that the most important things worth saying about the unfinished agenda of the Department of Labor related almost entirely to the administration of the Department, and the *Report* concentrates on that topic. I still believe that the most important thing that ought to be done is to improve the administrative efficiency of the department. Indeed I believe that it presents more promise and potential of administrative strength than any other department of the government. Perhaps this is because it is small. It is not because of what I or any of the other secretaries who are here did, because all of us found that strength there when we began our service. I suspect that Jim Mitchell, who preceded Arthur Goldberg, did much to develop the department's administrative potential. What he did is very important to this country, perhaps as important as any of the department's policies.

I tried to speak about this potential when I discussed my unfinished agenda eight years ago. I described how various efforts were made "to develop a flow of ideas and suggestions up the line within the department. The prevailing notion is still that what is asked for will be supplied, but that volunteering anything from below isn't worthwhile. Better be quiet is the attitude than to risk being wrong." It is a shame that our government agencies are often run on that basis.

The report goes on: "Written communication in the department suffers seriously from arthritis complicated by delegation. When most of what is written is prepared by someone other than the signer, the writer assumes only ersatz responsibility. He or she says the least that is required, burying it for protection in as much verbiage as the traffic will bear. Most sentences are long. Three or four ideas are loaded in to increase the odds that one will be impressive and that if another is wrong it will get lost. The department's effectiveness would be doubled if its prose were cut in half, if those who initialed documents read them, and if those who signed them wrote some of them." My unfinished agenda is really a list of improvements that could be made in the operation of the Labor Department.

I concluded my report with eight substantive matters that I still think important. Not one of them involves collective bargaining, although part of the report did deal with the question of collective bargaining within the federal establishment, which is still a terribly important problem. The omission of any other reference to collective bargaining perhaps reflects the fact that collective bargaining was an acquired taste with me. I had a great respect for it, but I never understood it. Someone ought to figure out what is in the genes of our society that produces the miracle of collective bargaining. One way or another, most collective-bargaining disputes get worked out. The cost and loss of that process are nothing more than an occasional kick in the shins. Moreover, the Taft-Hartley Act, which we all agreed was absolutely intolerable when it was passed in 1947, has never been amended in a single respect as far as the collective-bargaining process is concerned. But I did not discuss collective bargaining in my report then and shall say no more about it now. I shall turn to the eight points I did mention.

Item number one concerns the failure of the strong effort we undertook in 1968 to stimulate national and congressional concern about worker fatalities and occupational disease. We took care of that item when we passed the Occupational Safety and Health Act in 1970, so I shall move on to the next item.

Item number two concerns the unemployment-insurance laws, which remain substantially what they were a third of a century ago. The barnacles on them have become rebukes to legislative and administrative responsibility. Although some changes in the laws have been made, the barnacles still remain and, under the pressure of changing circumstances, have become worse. I think the present theory underlying unemployment compensation is totally wrong. It is entirely remedial when it ought to be preventive. For example, in West Germany and France, a good part of the unemployment-compensation fund is spent to grant up to two years' leave of absence for people who need retraining when they are threatened with displacement by a machine.

Item number three concerns the Taft-Hartley Act. I said, "The protections of the Taft-Hartley Act have not been extended to those areas in which they are most needed—

agricultural and not-for-profit enterprise. . . . Section 14(b) and situs picketing flaws still remain." I have considerable confidence that something will now be done about these issues.

Item number four has to do with the bracero program. There is a note of self-congratulation in the report, since at the time it was written there were no braceros in this country. There are no braceros now, but the satisfaction that came from getting the braceros out has turned to paste in my mouth. I guess it would have been better to let them come in on a contract basis than to do what has been done since the law has been enforced. I certainly would put on my agenda today to do something about the six to eight million aliens in this country, who live and work under unsatisfactory conditions. When I am told it is impossible to police the situation, I say, "Nuts!"

Item number five concerns our employment statistics: "The definition and measurement of unemployment has not been changed significantly during the past five years or during the past fifteen. More broadly, social indicators were not developed to complement the economic indicators, and since we do only what we measure, the measuring principally of economic facts continues to contribute to a distortion of program emphasis." The measures of employment and unemployment, which are compiled by the Bureau of Labor Statistics, reflect a nationwide averaging of successes and failures and so conceal the condition of those remaining at the bottom. These statistics tell the economists what they need to know about the working of the system and provide balm for the egos of administrators, but they report only implicitly and incompletely on the human condition. Their worst defect is that they encourage taking satisfaction from current accomplishment if it is better than past performance without inquiring whether that past had validity as a basis for comparison. It would be high on my list of priorities today to see that something is done to revise the measurements of employment and unemployment, work and leisure, education and training, and other social indicators that are used in this country. We cannot continue to rely on taking snapshots each year or each month of a particular condition and pretending that we get a complete and accurate picture from the overlay of those snapshots. When we develop some longitudinal measurements of what is happening to people in this country, especially as they move from education and training to work, we will begin to know something about our manpower and training programs. Until we do, we will have no basis for a cost-effective analysis of those programs.

Item number six in my January 1969 report said, "Youth unemployment remains twice the adult rate and, among minority groups, an incriminating 20 to 25 percent." Those figures have just about doubled in the last ten years. I am currently devoting all my energies to this particular problem. Manpower policy seems to me to make sense only if it is tied to educational policy. Linking manpower and educational policy has important implications for the structure of the federal government. I think that youth unemployment, including the underemployment of college graduates, is among the most serious problems we face in this country today.

Our current unemployment figure is barely tolerable, and yet we maintain it only by turning more and more older people out to pasture at a younger and younger age and by postponing the time when younger people come into the workforce. We must finally face up to the absurdity of dividing life into three time-traps: youth for education, maturity for work, and old age for the denial of either of those privileges. We must realize that there is an interweaving of work and education that will give us a better answer to the "manpower" problem.

The seventh item was stated this way: "The Department of Labor is not yet an effective participant in economic policy formulation within the administration." That is a terribly important point. Of the seven secretaries who have served since

1960, I think that only three—Arthur Goldberg, George Shultz, and John Dunlop—have been intimate participants in economic policy formulation. I think it terribly important that the economic policy of this country be the product not just of the Council of Economic Advisors but also of those who bring to the councils of government the practical understanding and the range of acquaintanceships that usually result from being secretary of labor and secretary of commerce.

The last item on the agenda I drew up in January 1969 reads very simply. It is at the end of a list called, "Some Illustrative Suggestions of the Disappointment, Frustrations, and Failures of These Past Five years." The last item is, "November 5, 1968," and that was the day that Hubert Humphrey lost the election.

George P. Shultz
(1969–1970)

George Shultz was born in 1920, was educated at Princeton University where he received his B.A., served in the marines during World War II, and then came to MIT where he received his Ph.D. in economics with an industrial-relations emphasis in 1949. He stayed on as a member of the faculty until 1957 when he left to join the University of Chicago Business School, first as professor and then as dean.

In 1969 he was named secretary of labor and served until he was appointed director of the newly created Office of Management and Budget. In 1972 he was appointed secretary of the treasury and assistant to the president. In 1974 he left office to become president of the Bechtel Corporation.

I shall offer here a few observations which I hope will be suggestive, though they will certainly not be definitive.

First a word about the Department of Labor. It is relatively small as government departments go, yet it is by now extremely important. A very large sum of money is administered, especially in the manpower programs. Responsibility for labor-market institutions and unemployment insurance rests there, a very large body of regulations is administered in the department, and the general influence of the secretary of labor on the world of work and labor relations can be immense.

With this importance in mind, I have found it interesting to review the evolution of the department. It is my impression that in the years following World War II the department and the secretary's office formed a sort of political base through which the administration kept in touch with the labor movement. If it was not labor's department, that may have been due to an uncertainty as to which branch of the labor movement was the real owner.

Particularly beginning with Jim Mitchell, the department enhanced its stature as a professional organization, though Jim managed under difficult circumstances to develop strong personal good will and communications with the labor movement. As I viewed it in 1969, this emphasis on professionalism had been reinforced by Arthur Goldberg and Willard Wirtz, and the department had achieved a kind of bipartisan standing. By the nature of the case, it seems to me that the department should always be a real "swinging outfit," ready to get into the important problems of the day. At the same time it will proceed with the surest foot if its base is securely professional and its homework is well done.

So my first suggestion is to preserve that bipartisan commitment to professionalism. This admonition certainly applies to all of the tasks involved in the regulatory aspects of the department's work, and here I think a special contribution can be made. Secretaries of labor and those who work with them in the department, whether presidential appointees or civil servants, tend to be interested in and have a real feel for the way labor and management and other labor-market institutions behave. There is an obligation to build on that special understanding a somewhat different pattern of regulations than is found elsewhere in the government. The most thoughtful and penetrating discussion of this proposition that I have seen, as is true in many other areas as well, is the paper written by John Dunlop during his tenure as secretary under the title, "The Limits of Legal Compulsion."

The system of private collective bargaining is in pretty good shape right now. It has even been quite a while since the *New York Times* pronounced the system bankrupt. We have not had an emergency dispute in a long while, and the system has done an outstanding job of developing both a consensus on the rules of particular workplaces and consent to the contractual arrangements made. This record has been particularly striking during the late 1960s and 1970s, when so many institutions have been in turmoil.

I continue to believe that the best policy for the secretary with regard to private-sector collective bargaining is to stay out of the way, to point the parties toward the Mediation Service when help is needed, and to counsel with the parties well in advance of potential crises so that everything possible is done to arrange an appropriate environment for bargaining. The responsibility for conducting the bargaining should remain with the parties. Sometimes it will have to be forced upon them, but the contract will have its greatest acceptance if the parties know that it was, in the end, their responsibility.

I recognize that this approach implies a degree of tolerance of strikes—a willingness to say in so many words that strikes are not intolerable, that they do not evidence a breakdown in the system, and that, on the whole, the damage to third parties is almost always vastly overestimated. The secretary will have to say this, not only publicly, but also to puzzled colleagues in the cabinet and the White House as well as to impatient senators and congressmen.

As important an issue as any facing the country today involves the system, or perhaps we should say lack of system, for income maintenance. The country is spending a great deal of money, which in itself is okay, but what we have for it is a patchwork at best and a real shambles in too many respects. There is no coherence to the way in which people in need get money from the government. There are tremendous inequities among recipients, especially between the working poor and those not working, and there are very undesirable messages carried by the high and sometimes confiscatory rates of taxation that apply all too often to the benefit structure taken as a whole.

The department has the direct responsibility for an important segment of this system. In fact, it can certainly be argued that the traditional system of unemployment insurance, especially if expanded appropriately, in coverage and with federally mandated benefit levels, is the soundest part of the system. I fear, however, that the many amendments that have extended the duration of benefits and the large flow of federal funds from the general treasury have drastically changed this system. I might say that the social-security system also seems to me to be entering a stage at which a drastic change in concept is needed.

At any rate, it is high time that all the income-maintenance programs—AFDC, SSI, food stamps, and so on—were considered as a group and drastically overhauled. I hope the time has come for a negative income-tax system tied conceptually and administratively to the positive tax system. Since the labor market, its people, and its operations are so intimately involved, it seems to me that the secretary of labor and representatives of the labor movement have a strong and necessary role to play in the revisions I hope will take place.

Every secretary of labor here has worried about and worked hard on the tremendous problem of unemployment among teenagers, especially those living in the central cities. We know that the problem is severe even in times of strong labor markets, so it involves more than just the availability of jobs and the acquisition of basic skills, important as these dimensions are. Schooling, housing, and transportation are a few other aspects of the problem.

I continue to feel that the high and undifferentiated minimum wage is in part responsible. Perhaps the social-security tax should not be assessed on that portion of payroll that constitutes wages paid to those under nineteen years of age. Surely we have learned a lot from the many efforts to deal with this problem, but we are nowhere near the answer. Perhaps it is one of those problems that cannot be solved but must be always tended. In some ways the greatest successes have been achieved in so-called experiments, although these often lose their fire when the experimental period gives way to a well-organized effort. Maybe we need a continual experimental mode in programming for this area.

James D. Hodgson
(1970–1973)

James D. Hodgson was born in 1915, received his B.A. in 1938 from the University of Minnesota, and did graduate work there and at UCLA. In 1941 he joined the Lockheed Aircraft Corporation, rising eventually to the position of corporate vice-president for labor relations. In late 1968 he joined George Shultz in Washington and served as undersecretary of labor until 1970, when he was appointed secretary after Shultz moved to OMB.

In 1973 Hodgson returned to Lockheed as senior vice-president, but he resumed his public service when he was appointed ambassador to Japan in July 1974, a post he held until January 1977.

I should like to discuss some of my observations on Japanese labor. While this subject lies somewhat outside the stated purpose of this conference, the contrast may add some perspective to our discussions.

Although I thought I knew something about the subject of men and work, I found Japan a wholly unsettling experience.

On the other side of the world, things in the world of work often seem upside-down. I suppose I would have to say that humility normally tends to come hard with me, but during my stay in Japan it came quickly and ruthlessly. What is one to think, for instance, of a nation where equal pay for equal work is neither practiced nor sought, where unions bargain to raise the retirement age and repeatedly vote against a shorter work-week, where 2 percent is considered a dangerously high unemployment level, where young workers actually have lower than average unemployment, where workers are promoted by group length of service rather than by demonstrated individual competence, where productivity and pay levels are almost never related, and, finally, where individual initiative among workers is discouraged as being unsuitably disharmonious?

After digesting all these strange facts, I turned my attention to the Japanese union movement. There I found so-called enterprise unions, but since I wasn't born yesterday, I knew these were really company unions and obvious patsies for the clever oriental managers. Obvious, at least, until I watched these same unions in three successive years extract wage gains of 22 percent, 34 percent, and 14 percent from their reluctant bosses, more than twice as much as their American brethren gained in those same years.

I found myself thinking, "These unions must strike often and long to achieve such whopping increases," but I discovered that I could barely read the percentage figure of man-hours lost to strikes because it has so many zeros after the decimal point. About then I learned that in Japan three days is considered a long strike and, furthermore, that a strike is never staged without plenty of advance notice and a meticulous identification of the time and place of its start. This is all done so as not to inconvenience anyone, especially not the management. Later I came to understand that in Japan the unionist's most effective strike weapon is to appear on the job wearing a red armband. This causes such an embarrassing loss of face for the boss that he tries to sneak into his office through the rear entrance and won't even come out to go to the restroom during the day. So it goes.

This was a learning experience for me, but perhaps it was even more an "unlearning" experience. As chastened as I was, I tried to develop a deeper understanding of this curious society, which, though it evidently does not know Western rules, seems to win all the games, at least all the games in the global economic big leagues. My search for enlightenment led me to recall that American society is first and foremost dedicated to the venerable Judeo-Christian objective of justice. The Japanese, however, spurn justice as a priority and instead seek harmony. We American justice-seekers think in terms of rights. The Japanese do not. Instead, the Japanese stress *relations* and in so doing reflect the quaint notion that an emphasis on individual rights is disharmonious. The distinction here is simple. In American life the individual strives to stand out. The Japanese, however, seeks to fit in, and fit in he does. In the United States we make a virtue of public controversy and the free competition of ideas. We make our policy decisions and settle our differences largely through adversary proceedings. The Japanese frown on "adversaryism" and seek, instead, consensus, as they have for centuries.

The Japanese do not consider 51 percent a majority, at least not a workable majority. They do not think they have consensus unless at least two-thirds of those involved are in agreement, and even then a bone must be tossed to the remaining third. Their attitudes about rights and justice might lead an observer to conclude that the Japanese have a certain indifference to the law. It is true that, by American standards, they have but little codified law. Neither do they have many lawyers, a sign of their limited sophistication perhaps. They actually have less than 10,000 lawyers for their 110 million people. We Americans outnumber them in lawyers per capita by twenty to one. All of this, of course, should produce a lawless society. What it does produce is the lowest crime rate of any civilized nation. Furthermore, there is no such thing as a jury trial. Even worse from a lawyer's point of view, nobody sues anybody in Japan. Business and labor contracts are somehow negotiated without lawyers.

The Japanese are out of date in many other ways as well. For example, in the world of romance, most marriages are still parentally arranged and last. Americans outrank the Japanese by ten to one in number of divorces. Since they have not yet caught up with modern educational methods, the Japanese literacy rate is the world's highest. In the last few years they have even passed Americans in longevity; their life expectancy is now second only to that of Sweden. Considering everything I have said, it may seem that I have come to regard the Japanese people as ten feet tall. They aren't quite that tall, though they have actually increased their average stature by almost four inches in just the last generation.

By now it should be readily apparent that I currently suffer from an advanced case of cultural shock. My diplomatic detour has taken me far afield from what passes for contemporary reality in the American labor scene. Therefore, I shall simply conclude my talk with a few observations on public policy for the world of work, Japanese-style.

I am impressed that these friendly Asian allies of ours have not found it desirable to emulate us in many ways. They have not undertaken extensive government manpower programs. They have neither invested large sums of their taxpayers' yen in government social programs nor built up much of a bureaucracy. Nevertheless, they have realized some fairly impressive manpower achievements.

I have in mind such achievements as nearly full employment in good times and bad, very little youth unemployment at any time, and a comparatively equitable distribution of national income among the citizenry. Pay disparity from top to bottom is far less in Japan than here. They have a commendably high level of job safety, a broadly and incredibly talented workforce, and a remarkably high level of worker job satisfaction. Surveys repeatedly show that 80 percent of the Japanese enjoy their work and do not want it changed.

In my opinion, there are three impressive reasons why Japan has not had to undertake much in the way of remedial and regulatory measures. First, uniformly the Japanese people like to work and take great pride in it. Their work ethic is unquestioned, and the worth of work is never challenged. Second, the Japanese who leaves school and enters the workplace invariably is equipped with full literacy—functional and otherwise—normally complemented by a usable, marketable skill. Third, not only do the Japanese enjoy work, they enjoy working together. Group harmony prevails in the workplace and elsewhere. Cooperation does not have to be encouraged; it is automatic. It seems to me that these are the three fundamental, underlying strengths of today's Japanese workforce: their attitude toward work, their preparation for entering the working world, and their capacity for working cooperatively.

It is often said that Japan is an unfortunate nation because it lacks resources, meaning of course natural resources. Japan keenly realizes this shortcoming, so it has placed its bets on another resource—the human resource—in its postwar march to the forefront of the modern economies of the free world. And it is in the superb quality of its human resources that Japan is probably the most enviable of nations.

John T. Dunlop
(1975–1976)

Born in 1914, John Dunlop completed his undergraduate and graduate education at the University of California. He joined the Harvard University economics faculty in 1938 and moved from teaching fellow to professor to dean of the Faculty of Arts and Sciences, the position he held when he was asked to serve as director of the Cost of Living Council in 1973. He was appointed secretary of labor in 1975.

Dunlop has served on a great many public boards and panels but is perhaps best known as the architect of the dispute-settlement machinery in the building and construction industry. He is the author of a number of major studies in wage determination, collective bargaining, and industrial-relations systems.

I take special satisfaction in being included here because all of the secretaries who have served since 1961 are people I knew before they held the secretary's post and with whom I worked with great pleasure while they held that office. Because of my relationship with the secretaries and because I myself was in the office so shortly, I do not know whether what I have to say constitutes an unfinished agenda of my own or is essentially a professorial view of the unfinished agenda in this area—a view I probably would hold even if I had never been the secretary of labor but drew only on my colleagues' experience.

I shall start by discussing three matters that are on the agenda of the administration and of society as a whole, but that involve the secretary of labor and the department in a significant way. Then I want to discuss six other items for which I think the department has a particular responsibility.

The first of the three general matters is the general state of the economy—the levels of employment and unemployment, the rate of economic growth, and the rate of inflation. The problems of the economy peculiarly affect the department— and the department, I think, has a major contribution to make to their solution—but they inherently involve the whole of government at the federal level and increasingly at the state and local levels as well. Leadership in this area, however, has to come from outside the Department of Labor.

The problem of the economy is the unfinished item that is probably at the top of all of our lists. But I want to suggest that a part of this problem, at least from the universities' point of view, involves leadership in ideas. The received ideas in this field, developed over the last generation, seem today quite sterile. The operation of our economy is much too complicated and the motivations of people in organizations and their aspirations are much too complex to be encompassed in a simple formula or econometric model. Such models often prescribe, in simplistic fashion, that more government money be spent or some other action be taken. Yet we still do not understand how jobs are created in our society, and developing that understanding should be on society's unfinished agenda.

We have created nearly 25 million jobs over the last 25 years. But if one asks an economist to explain the process of job creation, one finds that the state of our knowledge is very poor. We not only lack sufficient knowledge of the job-creation process, fundamentally we do not know how to mesh private and public policies to bring about the consensual set of conditions necessary for job creation. So this very first problem is most serious because it is not simply a matter of our knowing what to do but lacking the will to do it. Rather, we have arrived at a stage where we do not really know what to do about the economy.

The second general matter that involves the whole government is the problem of the low end of the wage scale or income ladder and its relationship to the welfare program, Medicaid and Medicare, housing assistance, and unemployment insurance. The interface between people who work and the transfer-payment system is something about which we know very little. In my mind, we do not have viable policies to deal with this issue. Again, however, I think that the Labor Department and the labor secretary are in a position to exercise leadership and to assume a position in a government that is often and understandably dominated by other concerns, including monetary policy, fiscal policy, and international considerations.

The third general topic that I want to mention was discussed by Willard Wirtz. I happen to think that throughout the federal government there is a need to attach a very high priority to the development of managerial and administrative capacities. At present there is a conflict among civil-service rules, collective-bargaining contracts (which now cover two-thirds of the federal workforce), and equal-employment-opportunity regulations. These conflicting rules create a state of mind that often makes it impossible for even the best set of managers to run even the most manageable programs. This is an urgent matter to which, in my opinion, no one in the government is giving serious thought.

These three basic matters cut across all departments of government, but they are so fundamental that they need to concern the secretary of labor. Now I shall turn to six issues that I perceive to be the responsibility peculiarly of the Department of Labor.

First on the list is the need in our society to stop playing with fads that are supposed to cure structural unemployment and other structural weaknesses in the labor market and begin the process, which might take at least a decade, of developing institutions to deal with those problems. The list of structural weaknesses includes the employment problems of young people, of minorities, and of women. There are also two other areas that need to be treated as structural problems.

First, we face enormously complicated regional employment problems in the country. Second, we have the problem—to use the diplomat's language—of "people without documents," or illegal aliens. Consider the regional employment problem, for example. In a number of northeastern states, a large sum of money is spent to train people for jobs, although employment is not increasing very much, if at all. Such training programs are likely to be much less successful than comparable programs in states like Texas or Oklahoma, where employment is increasing at a rapid rate. The notion that there is a uniform relation between dollars spent and jobs created is therefore not viable, in my opinion. Such estimates by the budget committees and by economists do not take into account regional differences in labor market conditions, differences in expectations, and differences in the financing of the expenditures.

We need to devote ourselves systematically and persistently to these structural problems in the labor market. In my judgment, over the last four or five years there has been a disposition on the part of large businesses and labor unions to concentrate on the youth employment problem and the minority employment problem and to adopt approaches that have not been tried before. My first departmental priority would be to launch a concerted attack on all these structural problems.

The second topic on my departmental agenda I would describe as leadership in the labor-management scene, and I would endorse the view that that leadership should be active. I do not necessarily mean that leadership requires involvement in a particular dispute. I do think that it requires dealing with the underlying structural problems of labor-management relationships, which vary enormously from sector to sector. What is true in the rubber tire industry may not be true in the construction industry, and what is true in the maritime industry may not be true in the cement industry, to pick a few cases where I have had some experience.

There may be some industries where one does not need to develop an active program but where one should identify the problems, develop data systems that provide information on comparative wages, benefits, productivity, output, and so forth, and work with the parties so there is a degree of confidence in the data that are developed. There is also the need, I think it is fair to say, for significant research that concentrates on various sectors. I imply no criticism when I say that, compared to a generation ago, the department has become so preoccupied with its regulatory function that its interest in labor-management relations has sharply declined. I regard that as an unhealthy state of affairs.

The third item on my departmental agenda is reform of the regulatory process. I do not say that the objectives of our legislation are poor: we *do* need safe working places; we *do* need viable pension plans; we *do* need affirmative action. But I think we have reached a stage where the legal model, which involves the process of promulgating regulations, the subsequent litigious activities, and the game-playing between the regulators and regulatees, has seriously interfered with the collective-bargaining process and the achievement of our social purposes. I regard it as fundamental that we try to find a way to reach our objectives without the costs of the present process. I am fond of pointing out that in 1940 the Labor Department administered 16 major statutes. In 1975 the Labor Department had 134 major statutes to administer. When Mr. Goldberg became secretary there were 6,000 employees in the department. There are now, I believe, about 14,000 employees. The problem is not so much the growth of employment in the department. It is a small department compared to others, especially HEW. A dominant item on the agenda, I think, is determining how the department can carry out its regulatory assignment—administer its regulations in the workplace and achieve its statutory objectives—without destroying the collective-bargaining process.

My fourth item has not been discussed very much by the other secretaries. Looking ahead, I regard the impact of foreign trade on the United States as a major matter of concern. I refer not only to the administration of the assistance aspects of the Trade Act of 1974, but also to the fundamental policies that are involved. Although this is a broad and controversial subject, I take the position that we must overhaul our basic thinking in this area.

Economists and their camp followers in the public policy area have for generations adopted the view that free trade is the right policy. In the press they would, of course, acknowledge that there are adjustment problems in moving from one "equilibrium position" to another and that now and then people who are affected by such adjustments need assistance. But their general outlook was fortified by observation of what has come to be called the "beggar-thy-neighbor" policy of the last great depression, under which one country raised its tariffs, another country to compete raised its tariffs further, and a third further still, thus reducing the total volume of trade and making everybody worse off. This is a legitimate concern.

Anyone who looks hard at the world, however, will find that there have come to be infinitely subtle and complicated ways in which a nation can subsidize its trade and its economy. It is often almost impossible to ferret out the ways in which these subsidies take place. Let me press that point. When a country decides that it will help a company—for example, furnish it with capital so it will not go out of business or so it can modernize its plants—what part of that activity should be treated as a subsidy for the purposes of international trade? Which forms of assistance should be considered legitimate and which should be considered subsidies for trade purposes? How are excise taxes to be treated? Or those regulations that prohibit layoffs and handle such benefits through the price structure? My point is that ascertaining what is "fair trade" is an extremely sophisticated and complicated problem. We are not equipped intellectually or administratively to deal with that problem in the modern world, and it is going to be a controversial issue over the next decade, I assure you.

Item five on my list concerns our participation in the International Labor Organization. In November 1975 Secretary Kissinger, under my instigation and with the complete endorsement of labor and management in this country, wrote a letter to the director-general of the ILO saying that the United States exercised its constitutional right to give notice of withdrawal in two years. We hoped that the ILO would become truer to its first principles, less politicized, and less alienated from its fundamental functions. Since that time there have been some signs that the objectives we sought are being achieved. We do, however, face a continuing challenge of developing an understanding around the world of what we—labor, management, and government—stand for in the ILO and related institutions, and we also need a greater degree of understanding within our own country of the purposes and usefulness of our participation in such organizations.

The last item on my agenda concerns the duty of the secretary of labor to explain to the public the central importance of collective bargaining and free trade unions in modern society. The department must provide leadership in this area. There are many people in America today who somehow think it might be possible to get rid of both labor unions and collective bargaining (and who spend time working for this end) and who honestly believe, I am persuaded, that society would be better off if these institutions did not exist. It seems to me that one of the functions of the secretary of labor is to articulate for our society and its changing workforce the indispensable role that a free labor movement plays in Western democratic societies.

William J. Usery, Jr.
(1976–1977)

William Usery was born in 1923 in Georgia. He worked as a machinist for a number of firms and rose in the International Association of Machinists and Aerospace Workers to the position of grand lodge representative, where he served for over a decade.

In 1961 he was named as the industrial union representative on the President's Missile Site Labor Commission and in 1968 became chairman of the Cape Kennedy Management Relations Council. He was named assistant secretary of labor for labor-management relations in 1969 and served in that position until 1973, when he was named director of the Federal Mediation and Conciliation Service. He was appointed secretary of labor in 1976 and served until the end of the Ford administration.

When Arthur Goldberg was introduced, I started thinking about how I got started on the road that led me to this spot. So many of us were deeply involved in the space program at Cape Canaveral. Justice Goldberg appointed me to the Missile Site committee. That is where I met John Dunlop and where I started my mediation activities. I was suppose to be an advocate, but I got more and more involved in mediation. I really got my education at the "College of Cape Canaveral." You learned labor relations very quickly there.

My colleagues have already discussed many of the items that I think are important. I would like to talk about just a couple of them briefly.

We all know that the charter of the Department of Labor was to foster and promote the general welfare of the wage earners of America. When the department was formed, it had less than 200 people and consisted of what is now the Bureau of Labor Statistics and the immigration service. It had one law to administer and that dealt with child labor. Today the department has close to 14,000 employees, located not only in Washington but throughout this country and, indeed, the world. The job of administering the department becomes more and more difficult every day. There are, of course, many laws to administer and enforce. The department even has about 100 people working in an anti–organized crime strike force.

So I am concerned about the management of the department. There are many hard-working, dedicated career people in the department who truly believe in its mission. But in recent years no secretary has been on the job long enough to get hold of the organization. It is like moving an iceberg—you cannot see whether you have moved it at all. Just when you find out the things you need to do, your turn is up. I am envious of Willard Wirtz, who had such a long tenure as secretary. Perhaps I would have had more successes if I had had the opportunity to hold the post for that period of time.

Managing the department and, indeed, managing the government were among my major concerns when I served in the cabinet. Cabinet officers come and go, and each is concerned about how his activities appear while he is in that role. He becomes busy with many things and doesn't consider what must be done in the long run to make the government function as effectively as it could and as it should.

I should also point out that the secretary of labor serves not only as a cabinet officer but also as a member of more than 30 commissions and boards. For example, he serves as a trustee of the social-security system, and that system now requires a great deal of attention. The secretary is also chairman of the board of the Pension Benefit Guaranty Corporation, created by ERISA as an independent corporation operating within the Labor Department, and that is almost a full-time job.

When President Carter said that each cabinet officer should read all the regulations issued by his department, I thought about how I am not a fast reader and realized that if I had had to read regulations night and day, I would have been able to do nothing else. The Department of Labor now has over 400 lawyers, and they are constantly figuring out how to write new regulations. We wanted to achieve safe and healthful conditions in the workplace, for example, but we have made it very complicated. We have only scratched the surface in the area of occupational health, though we have, I believe, had a tremendous impact in the area of job safety. The issue the secretary of labor faces is how to balance the need for jobs against the needs of the environment and the need for occupational safety and health.

Another matter that concerns me is collective bargaining for federal employees, in both the Department of Labor and throughout the government. When Arthur Goldberg was secretary, the first executive order dealing with the rights of federal employees to collective bargaining was issued. Since that time we have had two other executive orders and two amendments. It concerns me greatly that we have not looked closely at how collective bargaining within the federal government ought to be handled. There are now two and a half million employees in the federal government, and 68 percent belong to labor organizations. Negotiations often deal with such topics as whether carpets should be put in offices. It concerns me that we can become so bogged down with such issues that we never consider what we are really supposed to be delivering to the American people.

I am also concerned about the whole area of collective bargaining as it relates to public employees in general. That issue has been debated and discussed at length. A mishmash of methods are being used in this country to carry on collective bargaining for state and local employees. In the long run, I think, it will be unfortunate for us as a nation if we do not introduce some uniformity in this area.

We must also have a firm commitment to putting everybody who is willing and able to be employed in a job. We were able, in the 1960s, to place a man on the moon and return him safely to earth. We were able to do that because we had not only technology and knowhow but also commitment. We must have the same commitment in the employment area. It always concerns me when I meet people who are out of jobs, because, as we say down in Georgia, "It ain't been so long ago that I don't know exactly what it's like." So we must make a commitment to finding jobs for our people. The opportunity is there, and I think we can do it.

My real concern, when I was secretary of labor, was to try to get the department to be responsive to the needs and the aspirations of the American people, to do that with compassion and understanding, and to try to foster and promote our free collective-bargaining system.

F. Ray Marshall
(1977–   )

Ray Marshall was born in 1928; he received a bachelor's degree from Millsaps College in 1949, a master's degree from LSU in 1950, and a Ph.D. in economics from the University of California (Berkeley) in 1954. After holding a number of university positions, Marshall came to the University of Texas (Austin) as professor in the Department of Economics and became director of the Center for the Study of Human Resources at that university. Marshall's principal research interests were in human resources and labor markets and in international labor affairs. He moved to Washington when he was appointed secretary of labor in January 1977.

Our nation today faces many crucial issues affecting the state of industrial relations and our economy. One example of this unfinished business is the issue of whether to grant common situs picketing rights in the construction industry. This controversy has been passed on without resolution from labor secretary to labor secretary, indeed from president to president, for almost three decades. I hope to witness the expeditious settling of this issue during my tenure, so that it will no longer distract from what I consider more urgent priorities, including speeding recovery from recession and reducing unemployment.

With more than seven million Americans jobless, this administration's highest priority is to stimulate full recovery from economic recession and put people back to work. President Carter has asked the Congress to approve a comprehensive economic recovery plan. It calls for creating, by the end of fiscal 1978, hundreds of thousands of new federally funded public service and public works jobs. It would substantially increase the size and scope of existing employment and training programs serving such groups as youth, military veterans, and others with particularly high unemployment rates and unique job-market disadvantages. The president's proposals also include tax revisions and other measures to stimulate the economy now, while ensuring long-term economic growth and private-sector job creation in the future.

With a goal of balancing the federal budget by 1981 and the need to carry out expanded federal programs prudently, the administration's economic plan represents the maximum that we feel can be accomplished within a relatively short period of time. Yet our proposals remain flexible enough to adapt to changing conditions, if our constant monitoring of the economy indicates that more stimulus is needed.

Everyone can philosophically support the goal of full employment; few can agree on its definition. In my view, full employment is reached when every American who wants to work can find a job without searching too long. Until that situation becomes reality, we have much to do. And at a time when this nation lacks a supply of workers to fill many important jobs and has so many tasks undone, there is no excuse for putting the unemployed in make-work or useless occupations. Under the president's economic plan, we propose to increase the present 310,000 public service jobs to 725,000 by the end of fiscal 1978. The jobs we envision would put unemployed men and women to work in a number of vital areas—health and psychiatric care, maintenance of public parks and lands, energy conservation, and a host of other areas where labor shortages are now preventing socially useful functions from being performed.

The ultimate rejection of a person is placement in a meaningless job, for this communicates to that worker our lack of faith in his or her ability to make a productive contribution to society. Worthwhile public service employment is an important interim measure to reduce unemployment's current waste of perishable skills and talent. It also will help reduce the social cost of unemployment in terms of crime, suicide, and related tragedies that tend to increase among people idled involuntarily. Meanwhile, public service employment will help reduce the inflationary effect of allowing jobless people to remain idle when they could be contributing to national productivity.

Federally funded jobs programs are limited in their ability to attack the prolonged joblessness experienced by some groups in our labor force—those whose lack of skills and other disadvantages perpetuate higher-than-average unemployment rates even under the best of economic conditions. The unemployment rate among teenagers is now 18.5 percent. The rate for blacks and other minorities is 13.1 percent, and for minority youth, 37.2 percent. Military veterans aged 20–24 have a jobless rate of 15.8 percent. Carefully tailored programs are needed not only to supply employers with adequately trained workers as the economy improves, but to help these groups develop relevant, marketable skills in training programs closely linked with the private sector.

Youth unemployment is particularly severe and adversely affects the attitudes and workforce attachment of men and women early in their lives. During overall high unemployment, the young must compete with more experienced workers for available jobs. Too many teenagers lack any job training or possess education and training ill-fitted to employers' needs. As a first step toward alleviating this problem, the Carter administration is seeking substantial increases in youth-oriented training and employment programs. In addition to doubling Job Corps enrollment from its present 22,000 slots, the administration proposes three new youth initiatives.

First, a National Youth Conservation Corps, similar to the Civilian Conservation Corps of the 1930s, will be administered by the Labor Department through agreements with the U.S. Departments of Agriculture and the Interior in state parks and forests. It would employ young people aged 16 to 24 in conservation programs and in maintaining and improving these public lands, creating some 35,000 jobs over the next 18 months.

In addition, a Youth Community Conservation and Improvement Project, developed by state and local governments under the Comprehensive Employment and Training Act (CETA), would employ youth aged 16 to 19 in such socially useful projects as neighborhood and community improvement and natural resources restoration and maintenance. These projects, in both urban and rural areas of greatest need, would create 30,000 additional jobs.

Finally, a Comprehensive Youth Employment and Training Program under CETA would enlist a full range of state and local employment services in providing young people with jobs and training. Programs will aim at helping disadvantaged or low-income Americans aged 16 to 21 who are out of school and out of work. Half of the $900 million to be spent on this effort would be allocated to CETA prime sponsors. The other half would be used by the department to encourage innovative and experimental programs for youth. These efforts would result in the creation of 138,000 additional jobs.

These measures can be accomplished promptly within existing program frameworks and will emphasize a broad range of job training efforts—apprenticeship, on-the-job training, and institutional education. New programs and, possibly, legislation will be examined for addressing longer-range solutions to youth employment.

In addition, the department has undertaken a major new initiative to expand apprenticeship training opportunities for the young, particularly minority group members and women. More than half of the existing apprenticeships are in the construction trades. The department is working with labor and management representatives to establish formal apprenticeship programs in industries and occupations where they have not yet been tried.

The administration has also announced a new veterans' program. Our proposals will improve job opportunities for military veterans and will involve both private and public employment and training measures. Under a new HIRE (Help through Industrial Retraining and Employment) program, employers will receive incentives for hiring Vietnam-era veterans in the form of funds to help offset the costs of any training needed to make veterans more employable. Some 35 percent of all new public service jobs will be set aside for veterans. We also plan to establish outreach units staffed by disabled veterans in the 100 largest cities to concentrate on bringing disabled veterans into the mainstream of the labor market.

Discrimination against men and women for reasons unrelated to their productivity continues to rob many American workers of employment and advancement opportunities. Equal employment opportunity is easier to achieve in low-unemployment periods, but it can be done under any conditions with the legislation available to us if a sound affirmative-action policy is followed by government and private employers. Coupled with such a program is the necessity to prepare workers through sound training and retraining for jobs that affirmative action opens up for them.

Legislation may be needed to reform the federal government's overlapping enforcement of civil-rights regulations, but whatever is done in this regard, the Labor Department must be given a leading role. Equal employment opportunity imposes a recruitment obligation on employers that does not always conform to the availability of skills in their immediate labor markets. It is essential that federal enforcement of laws designed to increase job opportunities for qualified minority group members, women, veterans, and the handicapped be coordinated with employment and training programs that can supply such workers.

I do not favor reducing the number of federal contractors who must prepare written affirmative-action plans to comply with Executive Order 11246, as has been proposed. Instead of lowering the requirements, we should improve the regulations—simplify them, eliminate undue paperwork burdens on employers, and avoid overlapping enforcement of equal-opportunity regulations by federal agencies.

Among our regulatory programs, the Occupational Safety and Health Act (OSHA) and the Employee Retirement Income Security Act (ERISA) will be major targets in our efforts to simplify complex government regulatory programs and relieve unnecessary administrative and paperwork burdens on employers.

Public confidence needs to be restored in the OSHA program. Although we are still studying the problems in this area, it is apparent that unnecessary regulations must be eliminated and confusing requirements simplified. More of our resources need to be directed toward developing and speeding up the issuance of health standards, without compromising protections for worker safety.

We also must resolve the administrative difficulties associated with dual enforcement of ERISA by the Labor and Treasury Departments.

In another major department enforcement program, we are studying the impact on employment and prices of raising the federal minimum wage. We are also examining the feasibility of basing automatic increases on a wage index. Inflation has rendered the present $2.30-an-hour minimum totally unacceptable for the nation's workers. I do not favor enactment of subminimum wages for youth.

One of the department's long-standing needs has been for improved administration of the Davis-Bacon Act, which requires setting prevailing wage standards for construction projects in which the federal government is involved. The department is experimenting with the use of automatic data processing equipment in arriving at prevailing wage determinations. We also need to improve Davis-Bacon enforcement administratively, as experience has revealed lapses and inconsistencies among federal contracting agencies in enforcing this essential component of labor-standards protection for workers.

My general philosophy in carrying out laws entrusted to the department's enforcement is that no labor standard should become an element in competition. If employers want to become more competitive, they should improve productivity rather than cut labor standards.

As for collective bargaining, we must continue to seek new ways of strengthening this vital democratic process. At a time when our nation needs to step up productivity in the workplace and ensure harmonious labor-management relations, the right of workers to organize and bargain collectively needs, if anything, to be expanded. Today, many groups that could greatly benefit from collective bargaining are prevented from doing so by their exclusion from labor-relations legislation. Agricultural workers are a prime example and should be brought under the protection of the National Labor Relations Act or other mechanisms such as the California labor-relations act for farmworkers.

I support pending legislation to speed up representation elections and decision-making processes of the National Labor Relations Board, because justice delayed too often has resulted in justice denied for many workers.

In the public sector we face the problem of assuring that the interests of both labor and management are adequately protected in the bargaining process—that both sides have equal control. In the absence of the right to strike for public employees, the only viable alternative appears to be binding arbitration, with more attention also given to developing better alternative methods of resolving disputes and impasses, such as fact-finding and mediation.

In conclusion, in striving to meet all of the goals we have set for ourselves, government recognizes that it cannot succeed on its own. Progress and change occur only with the cooperation and full participation of all Americans, including labor, management, and the public.

INVITED COMMENTS

Stephen I. Schlossberg

Stephen I. Schlossberg has been with the United Auto Workers union since 1963, as associate general counsel and then general counsel, working out of the Washington office. He is a graduate of the University of Virginia and also of its law school. During his varied career, he has been an adjunct professor of law at Georgetown University, special assistant to the director of the Federal Mediation and Conciliation Service, partner in a Washington, D.C., law firm, director of organization for the International Ladies Garment Workers Union in the South, and manager of a department store in Roanoke, Virginia. He is the author of Organizing and the Law, *published by the Bureau of National Affairs in 1969.*

The problems that have been discussed by the secretaries are recurring problems; they go on from secretary to secretary. I guess the most important message we have received today is that our society is not out of the woods and we have a lot of problems left to solve. One of the most serious problems, it seems to me, is the problem of labor-law reform. I understand the need of our brothers in the building trades to get the common situs picketing bill passed and thereby achieve equality under the law with other unionists. I also agree with what the former secretaries have said about the mass of issues before us. But I was disappointed that there was not more emphasis on the problem of labor-law reform.

It is a tragedy, it seems to me, that despite the long relationship between the UAW and General Motors, the most vehement dispute we had with the corporation in our latest major negotiations was over an issue that we called the "Southern strategy." General Motors had opened plants in the Sun Belt—in this case, the southern part of the United States—in communities where the people were desperate for some kind of work, and GM had paid two and three dollars an hour less than the corporation paid in the mother plants. These plants were usually extensions of others that were organized.

It was saddening to find that in its plants in the Sun Belt, General Motors conducted really rough antiunion campaigns. For example, the company distributed the UAW seal with a hammer and sickle inside. That symbol has to be explained to a lot of workers, but once they understand it, it carries a rather sinister message. Another message that was easily transmitted was that in a black-and-white situation, bringing in the UAW would mean the mixing of the races in ways that southern workers were likely to resist. The company also suggested that if the UAW came into a situation that was either all black or all white, it would work against the interests of the workers who were already there. Then, of course, there was always the unspoken threat: Remember when GM wasn't here? Remember when in this town you worked from "kin" to "can't"—from "kin see" in the morning to "can't see" in the afternoon—on your uncle's farm, and how you starved to death? Now you may not be making what a General Motors worker makes in Indianapolis, Detroit, or anywhere else, but you are making $4.50 or $5.00 an hour, and that is a hell of a lot more than you made before this plant came to town. And why do you think GM came? Well, GM came because of the open spaces and because of the clean air and because of the lower real-estate costs and the lack of urban problems, but it also came because this was a docile labor supply. The inference was that if the labor supply stopped being docile and if it cost as much to make a Chevrolet or an electrical system in Monroe, Louisiana, as it does in Indianapolis, Indiana, why go to Monroe, Louisiana? We lost a couple of elections at Monroe because of those kinds of tactics. What we had to do was get a pledge of neutrality, and we got it.

General Motors was severely criticized by some of its colleagues in the Business Roundtable for giving us that pledge. The pledge said that GM was going to do what employers and enlightened western societies have done for years: really let the workers decide on their own whether or not they wanted a union.

We won that pledge not only for the UAW but for other unions that attempt to organize GM workers in new plants. And once the workers knew that General Motors was not going to move the plant and was not going to penalize them, and that they were not going to suffer because they voted for the union, the workers voted the union in.

Now I suggest that we had to do across the bargaining table a most remarkable thing that the law should have done: after 40 years of the National Labor Relations Act, workers should be able to get an election without coercion. There ought to be one law and one system of collective bargaining for the whole United States—South and North. I happen to think that the chances of passage of major labor reforms that will cut out these unconscionable delays in union elections are now excellent.

Let me give you another example. A plant called the Monroe

Auto Equipment Company, once located in Monroe, Michigan, moved to Hartwell, Georgia in the mid-1960s. The UAW has been organizing at the Hartwell plant for 13 years. During that period our organizers have been beaten by the local townspeople and thrown out of town while state troopers stood by and watched; the UAW has been hung in effigy in the town square; barbers and real-estate men have told the workers in the plant that if they sign a union card, they cannot expect to get service in the town; and the company has threatened the workers and fired their leaders. The case went to the Fifth Circuit Court three times, and the company finally was fined for contempt. The case went to the Supreme Court, then back to the Fifth Circuit, and it is now back before the NLRB, which is considering a new certification after thirteen years. The workers have held on to their allegiance to the union for that long. We cannot expect workers to do this very often because it is a herculean task, but the Hartwell workers have done it.

We cannot allow a situation where an employer, by resisting and by engaging in all kinds of dilatory tactics, can deny union representation long enough to kill any urge to have union representation. We either have a social compact in this country or we do not have it. That is the argument we use with General Motors. If both sides are not prepared to be responsible partners in the industrial community of this society, to build a product and build it well, to work together toward a decent, safe, secure workplace, and to provide some method for workers to vent and voice their grievances, we are in deep trouble.

Now we should not have had to extract a neutrality pledge from General Motors. We should have been bargaining with General Motors about such great issues as shortening the work week, upgrading wages and pensions, and improving our joint health and safety plans. We need improved health and safety plans because there are only 3,000 inspectors in the Labor

Department and they could not possibly handle the health and safety problems in the industrial community if unions and management did not responsibly try to handle those problems themselves. The victories we have had in the area of health and safety are unsung victories. Nevertheless, the joint labor-management committees on health and safety in our industry have produced sensational results. We train together and we work together. How can we do all those things and at the same time try to destroy one another as institutions in the Sun Belt?

There is now a strong feeling that the National Labor Relations Act after 40 years must at last be made to work. It must be used to promote collective bargaining, not to hinder unionization. The union movement, however, has more enemies from the far right today than it has ever had before. Our enemies are more articulate and better financed than they ever were before. They do not believe in collective bargaining. They do not believe in unions. They will latch onto any issue they can in an effort to destroy us as an institution. If they can do that, they will also destroy our society, because the union movement is an important pillar of this society.

But we have something else going for us now—and that something is Jimmy Carter. I really believe that, because he is a man of the South, he can go to the South and say, "We've got to make the Labor Act work. Southerners can now compete with any other section of the country without being nonunion and exploitative of human beings. You can compete on the basis of clean air, cheaper real estate, tax-free municipal bonds, and other subsidies to new factories provided by the taxpayers of your communities. You can compete on the basis that it is pleasant and cheaper to live in a warm climate because less fuel and energy are required."

The South can hold its own and can do it with pride. But it takes a southerner, I think, to convince them of that. That is why I am glad Ray Marshall talks with a southern accent. It is his South and it is Jimmy Carter's South and, I might add, it is my South because I come from Roanoke, Virginia. I believe the South can be brought into the national industrial community. That is my first priority, and I hope that the former secretaries, all of whom have meant so much to this country, will continue to help us as we try to help Secretary Marshall and President Carter achieve that objective.

William C. Mercer

William C. Mercer has been president of the New England Telephone Company since 1972. His career in the Bell System began with the Western Electric Company. He held earlier positions at New England Telephone, was vice-president for operations at the Indiana Bell Telephone Company, and was also vice-president for personnel with responsibilities that included labor relations at AT&T corporate headquarters in New York, prior to his return to New England in 1972.

I have been involved in labor relations at both New England Telephone and at AT&T corporate headquarters, and there is one thing that I have learned from my experience. George Shultz said in his comments that strikes are not intolerable and that their impact on the public is less than we are led to believe. I would not quarrel with that. On the other hand, I would also say that the real impact of strikes is not on the public but on the employees and on the relationship between management and labor after the strike is over. Long, lingering hard feelings develop as a result of strikes. Therefore, in my estimation, it is important for both management and labor to try to be more statesmanlike in dealing with each other and in negotiating contracts and, if it is at all possible, to avoid strikes that have long-lasting repercussions. I have also learned that it is a lot easier for both parties to precipitate a strike than it is to settle one.

Arthur Goldberg spoke about the need to safeguard and improve the collective-bargaining process. Certainly in larger organizations we have come a long way over the years in creating a reasonable basis for negotiating contracts. From the management standpoint, however, one of the things that disturbs me is that when unions prepare for bargaining, they inflate people's expectations about what can come out of those negotiations. Labor should look at this problem. We will be bargaining with the communications workers shortly, and I received on my desk a sort of grocery list of demands that the CWA will place on the Bell System. Somewhere within those three pages of demands there is a settlement. But the thing that worries me, as I look at that list, is that people come to expect far more than a company—regardless of what company it is—can possibly grant. Unfulfilled expectations leave a very bad taste in the mouths of employees, even if the final settlement is bargained in good faith and the workers make substantial gains, but gains that do not involve a price beyond what the company—and in the long run, the general public—can afford.

I would like to commend the comments by several of the former secretaries on the need for improved administration, particularly their emphasis on the matter of regulations in the Department of Labor. If there is one thing that is disturbing to those of us in industry, it is the tremendous amount of time and effort that goes into complying with federal regulations. When new acts are passed by Congress, such as the OSHAct, the people who are asked to administer them too often see them as hunting licenses. They are like hunters who go out during deer season and shoot at anything that moves. I think that people at the head of the Department of Labor can help establish an attitude on the part of those who administer the laws of working cooperatively with industry. After all, we are both parties of good will.

I do not think that anybody in industry has any argument with the intent of OSHA, which is to promote safety and health in the workplace. Early in the administration of both the EEO law and OSHA, however, an adversary position was established by those who administer the law. In the case of EEO, some of these problems are being worked out—we have come a long way since the early days. But OSHA is newer, and I would only suggest that the Department of Labor can play a major role in making sure that the attitudes of those who do the inspecting and work with industry to improve safety and health are consistent with the intent of the law.

I want to make one final comment concerning the common situs picketing bill, which was discussed and supported by most of the secretaries. There are ramifications of that bill that go far beyond the shutting down of a single construction site. They involve the ability of construction workers legally to picket and thereby shut down the business where the construction operation is taking place. This means that a whole body of employees outside the construction industry can be affected by a dispute within the construction industry. I do not think that many people are aware of this implication of the bill.

I will conclude these comments by stating my belief that if we could only bring a somewhat more harmonious attitude to our labor-management relations—to both our negotiations and our day-to-day administration of contracts—we would all be better off. As James Hodgson has pointed out, we can learn a lot from the Japanese on this score. Unfortunately, there is a tendency in American industry and labor to get stuck in adversary postures on certain kinds of issues. We feel that if we compromise, the other fellow will say, "Well, I beat you." We should recognize that once in a while both sides can bend a little and still come out ahead, rather than maintain adversary positions and carry the fight on and on. Eventually all such fights get resolved, but, again, the bad taste that remains is not conducive to good labor-management relations.

John H. Lyons

John H. Lyons has been president of the International Association of Bridge, Structural, and Ornamental Iron Workers, known as the Iron Workers union, since 1961. He became a member of the union in 1937 and, after service in the armed forces, worked in a number of jobs, including supervisory positions. He is a graduate of the famous Trade Union Fellows Program at Harvard University, where John Dunlop was his instructor. He has served as vice-president of both the Building and Construction Trades Department of the AFL-CIO and the Metal Trades Department since 1961. He has also been a vice-president and member of the executive board of the AFL-CIO since 1967.

John Dunlop pointed out that he served and worked with each former secretary of labor before, during, and after his term of service. In my present position, I have also worked with each of them, starting with Arthur Goldberg, who had been secretary for nine months when I was elected general president of the Iron Workers.

Arthur Goldberg and I first worked together on labor-relations problems at the missile sites. Arthur was faced with trying to fathom the difference between "new" construction and "prototype" construction, which was a unique term borrowed from the aircraft industry and applied to the construction work at the missile sites. Nobody else seemed to understand that difference either, including our members who used to picket the sites frequently.

That led to the development of the Missile Sites Commission, which did an incredible job of dealing with such problems. Arthur Goldberg, John Dunlop, and Bill Usery were all deeply involved in the early attempts to get that program to work. Indeed, the Missile Sites Commission was successful in making collective bargaining work within the framework of a brand-new endeavor in our country.

When Willard Wirtz was secretary of labor in the Kennedy administration, new manpower legislation was passed that involved a certain amount of regulation. I was appointed to an advisory manpower policy commission, on which I still serve. Bill's longer tenure in office put him in a position to understand the problems involved in developing effective manpower training programs in the United States. I have concluded on the basis of my service that the difficulties we faced in the industry then are still present and, indeed, have grown worse.

When John Dunlop became secretary of labor, he decided that, because of his long experience in the construction industry, one of his prime goals would be to face up to the task of improving collective bargaining in the industry. He strongly supported the common situs picketing bill, which for 24 years had been bottled up in the committees of Congress. He decided to seek legislation to solve the problems of this industry, which is the largest in the United States. That legislation is, of course, again one of the key issues facing Congress today.

I want to say that the people of America who listen to the

media and to the opponents of the situs picketing bill have received a great misconception about what the bill allows. The bill that is currently on the floor of the House does not allow what many people have been saying it does. I want to say to my good friend from New England Telephone that the bill absolutely does not allow the expansion of a construction-site picket line off the construction site. That cannot happen within the framework of the proposed law. The proposed law merely corrects a legal misinterpretation of what is a secondary boycott. The Supreme Court's conclusion that a secondary boycott could occur on a single site of construction was incorrect. The employers on a construction site do not have a secondary relationship among themselves in any way, shape, or form. Whatever happens with respect to the labor relations of one employer on a construction site involves every other employer on that site. The employer who comes on the site with a specific history of labor relations brings with him the possibility of generating a problem for every other employer on that site. It is not a secondary relationship because every one of the subcontractors involved is closely interrelated with every other subcontractor.

Now, of course, every expansion of an existing plant creates a construction site. But because of existing interpretations of the law, a picket line set up at a separate gate that leads into the area where the plant expansion is being undertaken cannot be extended to a gate used by nonconstruction employees to enter the established plant. It just cannot happen.

I did not mean to divert so much attention to this issue. Of course, common situs picketing happens to be at the heart of one of our greatest efforts today: to improve collective bargaining in the construction industry.

Many of these problems are carried forward from one secretary of labor to another. We still have the manpower problem. We still have the equal-employment problem. We still have the collective-bargaining problem. We still have the productivity problem. And we still have the regulatory problem.

Each of the former secretaries of labor, in addition to addressing himself to the importance of collective bargaining, stressed the importance of the regulatory process and expressed concerns about overregulation. I was impressed with the statistics that Jim Hodgson quoted about the low number of lawyers in Japan. I have nothing against lawyers. But I have been told that there are as many students in law school today as there are lawyers practicing. For me, that fact poses an awful lot of problems with respect to the future of the regulatory process. Those lawyers will have to seek employment somewhere. Now I hope that our laws are not undermined because of a failure to enforce them. But I also hope that an excess of lawyers won't lead to overregulation.

Consider the iron workers' trade, for example. At the root of the history of our trade is the problem of safety. Our organization was formed over 80 years ago for the purpose of achieving job safety. As a group of employees, we put together our own safety regulations. Now we certainly believe in OSHA and support most of the regulations it issues, but we are concerned about certain regulations that are presumably designed to correct dangerous situations arising in our trade. I am going to note a single instance: one simply cannot erect structural steel without the employees, at some time or another, being placed in a dangerous situation. That is why we stress the skill of the employee. But the development of OSHA regulations with respect to the iron workers' trade could result some day in the government saying, "You have to stop using structural steel. It is too dangerous. There is no way to safely erect structural steel." Well, if you overregulate, that is exactly what could happen. Of course, sometimes you have to stretch a point seriously to see all the implications. But overregulation is as serious a problem as underregulation.

In the area of other regulatory laws, ERISA is extremely important. That law was designed for the very meritorious purpose of ensuring that every worker gets the pension he or she deserves. But ERISA is one of the most complex laws that the secretary of labor must administer—possibly as complex as the tax code. Moreover, the results of that regulatory effort have already seriously undermined the expansion of pension programs. Is it the objective of ERISA to cut down on pension plans? To make it difficult for workers to negotiate new pension plans? Does that result constitute successful regulation?

ERISA increases the costs of maintaining a pension program. Under most pension programs contributions are negotiated, not the end pension. ERISA's effect of increasing the costs of administering a plan therefore results in decreasing the benefits that a member gets from his contributions. Otherwise the member has to take more money out of his own pocket to get the same end benefit. This is a problem created by the weaknesses of the regulatory approach, and one the secretary of labor will have to resolve in the future.

There have been very few words today regarding what I consider one of the most serious problems our secretary of labor faces in the immediate future. That is the ability of the United States to achieve desirable environmental results without hampering the ability of our business organizations to expand. Just recently Dow Chemical spent $400 million in three years trying to build a plant in California pasture land in a relatively industrialized area. The corporation finally gave up and moved the greatest portion of that $400 million expansion overseas. A minor portion went to two other facilities within the United States. When control of the environment pushes jobs out of the country, I do not think we are gaining the results that we want or are taking a balanced approach to that subject.

Finally, there is one more subject that faces our future secretaries of labor, and it was touched on by John Dunlop.

So-called fair trade is creating pressures that are moving jobs out of the country. In many instances, it really is not fair trade. We must cope with the effects of such trade on the structure of collective bargaining in the United States.

Dale D. Stone

Dale D. Stone came to the former Sun Oil Company in 1969 from the Sunray DX Company, which merged with Sun Oil some years ago. He served as Sun Oil's vice-president for human resources before he assumed his present position as senior vice-president of what is now called the Sun Company.

I can't resist starting off with a few comments about Ray Marshall's message. I am very disturbed that he is willing to dismiss the common situs picketing issue so quickly in order to get on with more important issues. Reference has been made to the fact that this issue has been unresolved for too long. I thought it *was* resolved. I am not going to go into common situs picketing because it has already been amply debated, but I am disturbed about the approach that our current secretary is taking to that issue.

I can agree with him on the issue of regulation. There is too much regulation. The nature of regulation is an issue that requires much more public debate, and I am concerned that the government's approach to resolving the issue will be more regulation. The one point that I can really agree with is the concern about paperwork imposed on business by the Labor Department.

In the course of the discussion, there has been one disturbing thought that has run through my mind: I am not sure where our concern for the individual employee is in all of the debate and discussion that we have been having. By "individual employee" I do not mean just the laborer; I mean you and me and everybody who is employed in a structured system that has evolved over many years and has produced great things for this nation and great things for the individuals who have participated in it. We happen to feel in our Company that the greatest potential for growth in the future lies in freeing up the productive capacity of the individual that is currently not being tapped or used wisely. Within our company's system we are trying to develop those kinds of philosophies among our management and supervisors and those kinds of processes that will free up the productive capacity of individuals, take them out of the boxes they have been in, and give them the opportunity to contribute their full capacity to our nation's growth.

We hear a lot lately about the "alienation of the worker" and the worker's "inalienable right" to greater kinds of job satisfaction than he is currently getting. As I see the future, that alienation is going to challenge both the hierarchical system by which we manage our private enterprises and the structure of labor organizations themselves. Therefore I suggest that labor and management have a joint concern for the individual and that we should not let him drop out of sight while we debate situs picketing, or Section 14(b), or the role of the Labor Department.

I would like to identify, without going into any great detail, some public policy issues that I think the Labor Department needs to be concerned with and that we as Americans need to be concerned with. I want to identify these as *public* policy issues, not as issues that involve labor versus management versus government.

One is the issue of labor-law reform. The nature of the bargaining process is changing, and we do not sufficiently understand what is taking place. To begin now to address problems of the bargaining process with what either labor or management might currently perceive as desirable kinds of labor-law reform is a mistake. I think we need a great deal more understanding of the social forces that are changing the bargaining process before we can undertake labor-law reform.

Unquestionably, there has been a shift in balance of the bargaining process, with labor gaining greater strength. Labor seeks even greater strength through the current administration with bills that have been introduced and bills that they hope will be introduced. I do not know what that balance of power should be. From where I am sitting, I think it is already too unequal—but I could be wrong. For the sake of America, I think we need much more public policy debate on the issue of the balance of power between labor and management. I think we need to get a better understanding of the tripartite nature of the relationships among labor, management, and government and of how those relationships will be shifting over time.

I was disturbed by John Dunlop's description of what he feels the role of the Labor Department is and should be. Perhaps this is because I do not thoroughly understand his position, and perhaps because I see some implications in it that I do not understand. But I do not think that the role of the Labor Department can be defined and debated without including in that debate the role of the cabinet as a whole. There has been talk about which constituencies the cabinet officers represent and which they do not represent. I would hope they represent Americans.

I think there needs to be a great deal more public debate over the nation's energy problems, and, being from a company that deals mostly with energy, I cannot help bringing this issue in. I think labor has a great deal more at stake on this issue than is currently acknowledged. I would like to see the Labor Department direct more of its efforts to helping us understand the role of labor in the energy area and the impact it can have over the long range. We have done enough studies to know that there is a direct relationship between energy consumption and job creation, but we do not know enough about the relationship.

Finally, I would just like to observe that there are just too many government programs that treat symptoms and not real problems. I do not profess to know what the real problems are, but many examples have been cited here about the effects of such regulatory legislation as the OSHAct and ERISA. Many of the effects of these regulations were clearly not expected when they were first promulgated.

I think that the unemployment problem is a classic example. Almost every speaker has made reference to the great need to do something about getting our people back to work and lowering the unemployment rate. I agree that this is a great need. But I think that we know less about the unemployment problem than we do about some of the other problems that we have tried to address in ways that have turned out to be bad for our nation.

One of the things that disturbs me, for example, is the Bureau of Labor Statistics. The statistics gathered on unemployment were put into the system for purposes other than making public policy decisions. Yet they are being used to make such decisions, and they tell us absolutely nothing about the nature of the unemployment problem.

Thomas R. Donahue

Thomas R. Donahue held a variety of posts with the then Building Service Employees Union in the 1940s and 1950s and for a period had an overseas assignment with the U.S. government. He became assistant to the president of the Building Service Employees Union in 1960 and in 1967 was appointed assistant secretary for labor-management relations in the U.S. Department of Labor, serving under Willard Wirtz. Leaving that position in 1969, he became executive secretary of the renamed Service Employees International Union for two years and then vice-president for two more. He has been executive assistant to George Meany since 1973.

The trade union movement is dedicated simply to the constant improvement of the human condition, and that is an unending agenda. It is always ahead of us and always very long. It includes at all times the specific improvement of the working and living conditions of our members and their families. It includes equally the general improvement of the conditions of life of all peoples everywhere. It includes freedom in all its forms. It includes opportunity in whatever form. It is an agenda that causes us to mount efforts around the world to help our fellow trade unionists and fellow workers build free, democratic, and effective trade unions. It is an agenda that leads us into the struggle to resolve grievances, to negotiate better contracts, to ensure safe workplaces, to protect pensions, to maximize everybody's efforts to enlarge industrial democracy and to improve the quality of work life.

That agenda leads us equally to Capitol Hill and the capitals of the 50 states to work for full employment, a sound economy, clean air, welfare reform, tax justice, child care, and the host of other proposals of what is this year a 10-page document of legislative concerns of the American labor movement.

We have developed a four-part legislative program in the labor-law area. The first part of that program deals with "unfinished legislative business," including situs picketing, the Energy Transportation Security Act, which is colloquially referred to as cargo-preference legislation, the Hatch Act, and strip mining. Versions of these bills were passed by the Congress last year and vetoed by the president.

The federation has examined that unfinished legislative business and has said to the congress and to the president, "Why don't we simply get on with the things on which the nation agreed last year?" We can simply redo them, and this time we have a president who will sign them. That really was our hope and our approach on situs picketing. Congress, in its wisdom, passed the bill last year, and we thought it would be passed this year. Instead, we are getting bogged down in another struggle. This is legislation designed to correct the inadequacies of an earlier statute and to answer the problem that the Supreme Court raised when it said that Congress had not been specific enough on this point. So we have asked the Congress to be specific.

There is more misinformation on the subject of situs picketing than on any other subject known to man. There is a game that I see being played every day in Washington. People sit around with paper and pencil and draw diagrams. ''Well, now, if we have a plant here and a building here and a road here and a highway there and a hospital over here, where can you picket? If you have a large plant site and two constructions, a warehouse and a garage, can you picket both?'' The game misses the essential point. What we are really talking about is trying to clarify the responsibilities of the person who decides he is going to have a building built and the person who is charged with building that building. We have been befuddled and confused, and our efforts to help workers have been thwarted over the years by the imposition of a dozen corporate veils between us and the general contractor, the person who orders the work to be done, and the corporation that orders the building built. We say, ''Let's stop that.''

The problem, I think, is that only the professionals in the labor-management field—and not all of them—understand the technical aspects of the law. It is a highly technical problem. Where is the plant gate? What is a secondary employer? It is the same problem, I think, that affects discussions of public-employee legislation or of the right to strike. Professionals in labor relations understand the part that some of these matters play in the total collective-bargaining process, but, unfortunately, these topics are not easily translated to the citizenry at large. They are too easy to characterize negatively, so that hackles are raised by phrases like situs picketing and cargo preference.

The second part of the federation's legislative program concerns minimum-wage legislation. We will make an effort to secure a $3.00-an-hour minimum wage and to establish an automatic mechanism that maintains the minimum wage at a point that is 60 percent of the average wage in manufacturing. There is great sympathy, I think, for that legislation in the Congress.

The third part of our program is labor-law reform. Steve Schlossberg has addressed himself to the need for reform, as have others, and I am not going to talk very much about it beyond saying that what we have tried to do in that legislation is to establish a fair chance for workers to organize, to streamline procedures and reduce delays, to provide effective remedies against violations of the law, and to repeal Section 14(B) of the Taft-Hartley Act and thereby provide a national standard for the negotiation of union security clauses. We do not see anything unusual in these proposals or anything that is worthy of the strong opposition of any professional in this field.

The fourth part of our program calls for extension of the National Labor Relations Act to those who are not currently covered: federal employees, state and local employees, and agricultural workers. Extension to federal employees will simply establish by statute the collective-bargaining rights that are now given to federal workers by executive order. The problem of extending and guaranteeing collective-bargaining rights to state and local government employees is an immensely complicated one—complicated particularly by the Supreme Court's *League of Cities* decision. We simply have to fashion the machinery by which that extension can be done, and we think there are ways of doing that. Finally, we want to talk about extending coverage of the National Labor Relations Act to the farmworkers in some appropriate fashion that is geared to meet the problems and conditions in their industry.

We could have included in our program lots more. We, too, have our wish list and there are many other changes that might be made in our basic labor statute that, in our view, would make collective bargaining more effective and would help our already established unions and bargaining units. But we simply made a decision that we ought to put other matters aside for a time. In effect, we have said that existing bargaining units and unions are getting along, can reasonably fend for themselves, and can deal with the inequities or inequalities in the law. We ought to concentrate our attention on the people who are not now organized and who do not have a fair opportunity to join unions and negotiate contracts. In a sense, we have decided to try to help those people who have nothing and to put aside for the moment the concerns of those who have something.

Andrew C. Sigler

Andrew C. Sigler has been president and chief executive officer of Champion International Corporation in New York since 1974. He was named president of Champion Woodlands in 1956, executive vice-president and director of Champion International in 1972, and president of the Champion Papers Division from 1972 to 1974, before assuming his present position.

I have been trying to figure out the position that I represent on this panel. Given my background, I should not be classified as a professional in labor-management relations. I think I will simply call myself a representative private-investment decision maker who has been trying to direct a company as it attempts to grow and develop the jobs that we need in the private sector.

I wish that Champion International were a household word, but it is not. It will help to explain my position if I offer some information about our company. We are in the forest-products business, and our sales will approach $4 billion this year. We employ about 55,000 people. We are essentially a U.S. company, but we have major operations in the United Kingdom, Brazil, and Canada and have just extricated ourselves from operations in Belgium.

Speaking from the position that I have described, I find that I do not disagree with most of what has been said here. As a matter of fact, I find a great deal of encouragement in what the six former secretaries have said. There were some things in the remarks prepared by Secretary Marshall that bothered me a bit, and I will comment on that in a minute.

I represent a southern company that is highly unionized. Many southern areas do have unions and also a good record in labor-management relations. I should note that we do not engage in industrywide bargaining. Rather, we bargain on a unit-by-unit basis, which puts us in a very different kind of position from many other corporations.

The experiences that I have had in the United Kingdom, Belgium, Canada, and to some extent Brazil have left a great impression on me. I am a great advocate of the free-enterprise system. If you try to manage a major business in those countries, I think you learn that the free-enterprise system is something that should not be destroyed. It has been effectively destroyed in many countries. I mentioned that we recently extricated ourselves from the paper business in Belgium. The basic industries of Belgium, and the paper industry in particular, are in effect bankrupt and are only barely kept alive. The government and people of Belgium did not understand that their policies would put 5,000 people out of work in the particular company that we operated. That is the end result of destroying the free-enterprise system.

The general economic health of this country depends on our basic industries and our ability to compete in the world. I am convinced that the unique ingredient we have is the partnership between management and labor unions. In this country both are part of the free-enterprise system. Willard Wirtz referred in his remarks to "the miracle of collective bargaining," and I thought it was a marvelous phrase. I sincerely believe it is a miracle. The unique partnership between labor and management in this country has created high levels of productivity and freedom and puts us in a position to be, by far, the strongest economic system in the world. In public we criticize ourselves quite a bit, but we do have the strongest system in the world today.

I am bothered by the inability of American business to articulate its position in a decent way to the public. I have thought an awful lot about this problem, and I do not really know what the answer is. Unfortunately, every time we try to deal with the problem, something comes along that makes us look absolutely awful. These individual situations are often generalized and make the entire business community look bad. I think it is an extremely complicated problem. Over the last couple of years the economy has often been the lead item on the evening news. When it is, the business community's illiteracy is displayed on the television screen. Business is not able to deal with this image of illiteracy.

I sincerely believe that the collective-bargaining system is what makes us strong. We should not destroy it through regulations. I do not believe that strikes are intolerable. Certainly they are not intolerable in our business. They help to maintain a fine balance between business and labor. They allow us to get at underlying issues. That is what the collective-bargaining system is all about.

Secretary Marshall and some other members of the administration seem to take the position that interruptions in economic activity are intolerable and that we must therefore look for some amazing thing that will allow us all to agree. I think that is impossible. We have gotten to where we are by pushing and shoving and developing a proper balance. It is that tug-of-war between labor and management that has led to higher productivity and other benefits.

I do not like the idea of government intervening in labor relations in an attempt to help us come up with a different way of handling problems. I did not hear that in any of the remarks made by the former secretaries this morning, which I found very encouraging, but I did hear it in Secretary Marshall's remarks. As someone has noted, however, a person has to be in a job for a little while before he truly understands the situation.

Now let me turn quickly to a few other subjects. From my perspective, the inflation we have suffered over the last couple of years and the threat of inflation in the future stem from the inability of basic industries to increase capacity sufficiently to take care of demand. Increasing our capacity depends on sustaining private investment. What is going to happen to private investment? The level of private investment is linked to job creation. Will there be enough private investment to create the jobs we need?

I think that private industry can do and has done a marvelous job of creating jobs for the large "employable" portion of the workforce. But it certainly has not shown an ability to take care of the special kinds of problems that certain groups in the labor force have, and I do not think that it can. That is an area where there has to be creative public involvement. The kinds of employment programs that we have tried in the past can be criticized, but the fact of the matter is that we have to try such programs and figure out a way to make them work. The private sector cannot solve these employment problems by itself.

There is a myth which says that, given an investment tax credit, business will rush out like some automaton and invest. It doesn't work like that. In the paper business, the time from the inception to the development of a new pulp mill, which costs between $300 and $400 million dollars, is five years. For at least the first 18 months of that period we are required to do environmental impact studies. The point is that when someone puts in a tax credit, you do not then run out and undertake a large investment project, especially if the tax credit may only last a year. It is nice to have the tax credit—it adds to the profitability of the company and in the long run to its ability to invest. But it certainly will not affect decision making right now. Tax incentives are important, but we must deal with all the factors that affect private capital development.

I think that the marketplace works. The vast majority of the products and services we produce are dealt with in an effective way through the give-and-take of the marketplace. I have lived with controls, and they just do not work. The system is too complex. I thought John Dunlop's comments about the complexity of the system were on the mark. We just do not know enough, and controls frighten me to death. That is why I do not think we can find a substitute for collective bargaining, which is an effective way to deal with wages in the same way that the market place deals with prices.

Probably enough has been said about OSHA and ERISA, but I would like to second John Lyon's comments about the silliness of OSHA regulations as they affect the problems of steel erection. Safety is a very difficult problem with which we must deal constantly. It is almost impossible to determine why one mill or plant has a marvelous safety record and another has a bad one. Safety does not really depend on railings and machine guards; it is a matter of people. Accidents may result from carelessness or bad supervision, but most of all they result from the attitudes people have. For that reason safety is infinitely complicated and cannot be legislated.

I feel a little differently about ERISA. ERISA has had a bad effect in that some of the smaller pension funds have ceased operating rather than meet the law's requirements. On the other hand, pension contributions and some pension funds have gotten so big that I think there had to be some sort of guidelines for them. It does not bother me very much to have ERISA regulations applied to office workers. It bothers me more to have the regulations applied to operating employees, because they create problems in the area of productivity and output.

I look at the general business situation in this country and at our economic strength compared with the rest of the world with a great deal of optimism. That optimism is based on the fact that, for all its idiosyncrasies, we have developed a workable program of collective bargaining, which is essentially a partnership between labor and management, that has allowed us to attain high levels of productivity and freedom. In my view, that is all there is to basic economics.

Without high productivity and freedom, we cannot compete with the Japanese. But despite the wonderful terms in which they have been described, we really can compete with the Japanese people and, particularly, with Japanese business. For all the complaining we do about construction costs and about the collective-bargaining process, it is still cheaper to build and run paper facilities here than in Japan. That is one of the wonderful things about the forest-products business. Trees are one of the most marvelous resources we have because they are renewable. Long-term projections for our business indicate that we will continue to be the most effective and efficient operator in the world.

FURTHER DISCUSSION

QUESTIONER: We have heard the terms "inflation" and "unemployment" mentioned many times today. I read in the press several weeks ago that George Meany allegedly had been conversing with President Carter and President Carter had asked whether Mr. Meany would involve himself with the unions in voluntary wage restraints. I am sure that reference was made to price restraints also. Mr. Meany was quoted as saying that he would not participate in voluntary restraints at all.

What alternatives do we have right now to these large wage increases of 8 to 12 percent? The teamsters' contract calls for an increase of 74 cents an hour. Employers can't take that and pass it on to the consumers. That would result in a reduction of services and would cause more unemployment.

What alternatives do we have to voluntary restraint?

MR. DONAHUE. I was going to interrupt to say that I would sign in a minute for 8 to 12 percent increases. A lot of our people are having a tough time and little success in negotiating those kinds of wage increases.

Let me clarify the reference though. Mr. Meany did not say that he would not cooperate in voluntary wage restraints. The reference was to a line that I think appears either in the president's economic message to the Congress or in the Council of Economic Advisors' Report to the Congress. There the president calls for a program of prior notification of wage and price increases. Mr. Meany simply said that that is impossible. How does one give prior notification? How does one give 30 days' prior notification of a wage increase that you negotiate 11:30 at night and that is to become effective the next morning or three days later?

So what we are being asked to do is not to give prior notification but to forego a wage increase for one month. Well, nobody is ready to do that.

What Mr. Meany said very specifically is that we will not cooperate in such a program of prior notification.

Now, as for voluntary wage restraints, the president has not gotten to that point. There is a side story about what Meany said to reporters in Florida. The reporters, as is their wont these days, rushed word up to their people in Washington, and the next morning the reporters went to the White House and asked, "Did you see what Mr. Meany said? He said he wouldn't cooperate." The presidential press spokesman got trapped by the question. He made a statement that the president is not locked into any specific formula in his effort to minimize inflationary pressures and that the administration wants to have discussions with labor and management to see what can be worked out. Having said that, one of the newspaper guys said, "Well, does that mean the president is rejecting Mr. Meany's comments?" And the press spokesman said, "Yes."

The headline that night was, "Carter rejects Meany's statement." The next morning the reporters back in Florida asked

Mr. Meany at his press conference, "Mr. Meany, what do you think about President Carter's rejection of your statement?" Mr. Meany said, "I reject his rejection!"

But nobody has closed any doors on voluntary wage and price restraints. If the president wants to talk about voluntary restraints, we are prepared to sit and talk and try to do those things which are in everyone's interests. But it is, you know, an immense oversimplification to start with a position that says, "Now we are going to have prior notification." That is not going to solve anything and, speaking for the AFL-CIO, that puts an impossible burden on our unions. I suspect that it puts an equally impossible burden on employers, except that employers can schedule their increases. When we negotiate contracts, we of course cannot.

*   *   *

QUESTIONER: I would like both sides of the panel to comment on a problem that I consider nonadversary because it is so practical. That is the conflict between environment and jobs. Pressing for a better environment can cause a loss of jobs. We all know about plants that have closed down and communities that have, as a result, become ghost towns. This is such an enormous problem that I wonder if it could not be better solved by union and management people working together?

MR. SIGLER: Could I take a first crack at that?

We are in the pulp and paper business. I guess we encounter most of the kinds of problems that involve air and water.

We are today at a point where we have taken about 90 percent of the BOD out of our effluent and 95 percent of the particulates out of the air. These are the 1977 requirements.

I think you will find that most of us in industry are concerned about the year 1983, when the law says we must take it *all* out. Achieving that goal carries a high price. It will affect the expansion of investment and therefore will slow down the creation of jobs. The goal is also complicated by the bureaucracy needed to develop the environmental impact statements.

Stan Smith of International Paper tells about the work that was required to expand just one mill. The reports and documents his company was required to prepare took two years to complete and occupied nine feet of bookshelf space.

Now I can only speak with some knowledge about the paper business. We have seen the shutdown of some mills. Essentially the investment decision was made that if you had to pay the $2 million or $3 million to put in primary or secondary water treatment, the mills would be so uneconomic they could not survive. It is true that most of these mills did not have many jobs, but I feel very strongly that we have gone too far in quantifying the desirable levels of pollution in the air and water. We are reaching a point where the energy generation needed to run the equipment to take out the particulates and BOD creates more pollution than it eliminates. These are terrible problems to deal with. They have long-term job implications. And I am troubled by what has been done up to now.

MR. LYONS: Nobody that I know of in the labor movement really opposes the objective of improving the quality of water, the quality of air, and the quality of our environment. We are concerned, however, that the time frame within which we are supposed to achieve our environmental goals is unrealistic. We are afraid it is not a balanced approach and will destroy jobs. Clearly any type of operation that is a menace to health should be stopped, but otherwise our approach should be gradual and economically realistic, logical, and acceptable.

The problem is aggravated today by the fact that a very small percentage of the American population is very active in this field, and they are highly organized. They pursue extremely legalistic approaches in various parts of the country to achieve their objectives. For example, a small group of people—and a very large number of legal firms—are involved in the strip-mining issue. They will go to some part of the country where there is no mining activity and try to generate a court action that will result in a ruling that forbids strip mining in that area. No one else will be involved or interested in the court action in that part of the country. So the court issues a consent decree limiting strip mining, and this group then takes the decree to an area where there is mining and say, "Now, this is what the court has ruled."

We recently had a situation where a dam was 90 percent complete ($695 million had been invested in it) but was stopped by a small group of environmentalists because it threatened an endangered species called the "snail darter." This is a two-inch fish that we all used to identify as a minnow. That minnow they successfully placed on the endangered-species list and claimed that the dam would cause it to become extinct in this part of the country. It still exists somewhere else, and I have reason to suspect that it arrived in that part of the country in a jar belonging to the professor who is leading the fight!

MR. DONAHUE: I met the other day with the group of tuna fishermen from Puerto Rico who work on the West Coast. They have an impossible problem. They have a wonderful business that employs 35,000 people. The eastern spinner porpoise is on the endangered-species list and cannot be fished for or even caught unintentionally. So if, in taking in their tuna, the fishermen happen to catch in the net an eastern spinner, wittingly or unwittingly, they are subject to a $25,000 fine. As a result, they have shut down the tuna fleet. They are dealing with the problem the only way they know, and I suspect it is the way a lot of us would deal with it. They shut down the tuna fleet and said they are not going to fish any more because it is just too silly. They cannot work under these conditions.

Now the tuna fishermen have made substantial efforts to get the porpoises out of the nets, to redesign the nets, and so forth.

The fascinating thing about that kind of regulation is that it follows our fishing fleet wherever it goes. When the fleet is fishing down off Chile, our Coast Guard planes are still surveying the fleet's work. But next to our fishermen are the Portugese and the Japanese and the Russians, taking and killing all the porpoise they want. The regulation of the American fishing fleet therefore has no effect whatsoever in reducing the number of porpoises being killed, and yet we go ahead with the regulation.

There is a problem there to be dealt with, but imposing a zero limit on our fishing fleet is not the way to do it.

* * *

QUESTIONER: I would like to ask one of the secretaries to comment on the impending increase of the minimum wage. Won't it result in higher unemployment for inexperienced young people? If business has to pay higher increases to them, we will look for more experienced people and not hire high schoolers.

MR. DUNLOP: My feeling is that that sort of assertion is based on analytical models whose applicability to any given set of circumstances is questionable.

Now if you ask me, "Is it possible to raise the minimum wage of a country fast enough so that it would have an adverse effect on employment?" I guess human ingenuity could do that. But the relevant issue, it seems to me, might be addressed if you surveyed the rate of increase of minimum wages in this country since 1938, when the figure was first 25 cents an hour. One would have to conclude that it is an issue that is not so simple. That you could find someplace where, in fact, there have been adverse effects, I have no doubt.

On the other hand, you are really dealing with a dynamic situation in which technology, skills, training, enterprise, concentration, and employment are all changing. You must also deal with the very important question of how increases below the minimum wage are transmitted and transmuted above the minimum wage. And that is again a very complicated point.

So I guess the relevant issue is that one could probably not attribute any significant amount of unemployment generated over the period since 1938 to this factor, among all the factors that have been at work.

* * *

QUESTIONER: I would like to address my question to John Dunlop.

I have heard you say that collective bargaining ought to be pursued virgorously to try to settle some of the occupational safety and health issues, and you have been very active in that regard. I do not think that anyone would argue that that mechanism has been sufficiently exploited to yield the results it could. But I wonder if you would agree that we ought to pursue our goals through both collective bargaining *and* strict enforcement? I would argue that we must because of two factors: first, labor's inequality in terms of access to technical information, and second, the limits on the extent to which you can really control toxicity in the workplace without workers' active participation in the management of some of that technology—something that has been resisted very strongly, for example, by Shell Oil in the Oil, Chemical, and Atomic Workers' strike.

I wonder if, because of those two limiting factors, you are going to be able to push health issues, as opposed to safety issues, very far through collective bargaining.

MR. DUNLOP: It seems to me that, one, we make some advance in the general proposition concerning the use of collective bargaining if we distinguish different circumstances. Safety issues represent a different kind of situation, as Jack Lyons and other members of our panel have been saying.

On the health side, however, I think we do face the more serious problems because we really do not know very much.

One of the things we need is a data bank in this area. We have very different sources of data—there are 14 or 15 different agencies that have gathered a lot of information on health problems. One thing we ought to do is to arrange for experts from labor and management to review that information and to assume a greater role in how it is collected. If we expect people to have confidence in the data on which we are trying to build a regulatory system, we must have a greater degree of involvement and participation by both labor and management in the collection and analysis of the data, regardless of who is going to set the regulation. So that is one kind of role for joint action: data collection and data appraisal.

I think it is possible that in many cases the result of careful data appraisal would be government regulation. But it makes a difference whether a regulation derives from a kind of consensual analysis by parties who can give due regard to appropriate time frames and so on, or whether a regulation is the result—as it essentially is under the present process—of a bunch of government officers dealing with an area in which they have not had much experience and know very little. They put something out for comment instead of trying to encourage a practical solution to the problem. That process tends immediately to encourage both sides to take the most extreme positions in an attempt to influence the bureaucrats. When it is all done, our bureaucratic friends do not know any more about it than they did in the first place. And then the battle is only begun because we start through the courts, and that process takes a number of years. Furthermore, the courts do not look at these questions, in my view, on the merits. They look at them on certain kinds of constitutional grounds. Did the agency have the power to set the rule it did? Or did it have the right to interject itself into the jurisdiction of a state? Or did this guy have the right to appear as a party? They do not consider whether it was a good rule. In my experience the courts decide these matters very often on tangential and procedural matters.

In sum, sometimes the standard might be the result of discussion and even negotiation. At no time should a government administrator promulgate a standard or a rule, in my view, without having it put out for public comments so that everyone, whether he was involved in the discussions or not, has a free chance to state his own view. The administrator with the constitutional responsibility to review those comments should then see what the fair rule would be.

* * *

QUESTIONER: A great question that confronts us is that on most matters abutting the field of labor relations, we have proceeded along the judicial and legalistic path, whether one speaks of labor law itself or sundry other matters. How do we revamp American attitudes concerning adversary legalistic approaches to matters on which the legislatures or administrators have acted?

I am in favor of initial adventures toward joint decision making, but our whole system, it appears to me, is so penetrated by the concept of legalism that we have to wonder whether there is not a more fundamental question concerning our total strategic approach to this matter.

WILLARD WIRTZ: My reaction is one of quite basic sympathy. I think the only answer I can make to your question is that the law has walked in because "social nature," like "natural nature," abhors a vacuum. I do not think there is any defense to be made for the extent to which the law has taken over, not just the few things we are talking about here, but also the integration of schools, the development of the school system, and so on. I would not defend the process on any basis except to say that certain things had to be done by somebody and the courts have stepped in.

Now that cuts pretty deep. I guess the reason for the problem is that there are certain inexorable forces of change at work. It turns out that over the last 20 years the most traditionally conservative agency of the government, namely the law, has become the innovator in this society. On such issues as voting, the integration of schools, civil rights, and civil liberties, we see the courts rushing in and we wonder why. You try to figure it out and come to the conclusion—and this is the only answer I can live with when I get there—that the courts are insulated from the society at large. They are the most insulated branch of government because they are not elected.

The implications of what I have just suggested cast the whole democratic system into question. I have to believe that the only answer to the question raised is that the law is doing it because the forces of change require that some things be done. But it is a very bad bargain. If the other branches of government will take over and assert the responsibility that is needed, I think the courts will be so delighted to step aside that you will be unable to get out of their way as they leave.

I wish I were more confident that the legislative and the executive branches were going to face up to those responsibilities. I think it is more likely to happen at the local level than at the federal level, which is a terrible note on which to close.

CLOSING COMMENT

Charles A. Myers

In thinking about what has transpired today, I have been struck by the high degree of consensus evident in the discussions by the former secretaries. To be sure, there were different points of view on some issues, but I would like to note six areas of agreement.

First, the secretaries said almost unanimously that collective bargaining is working in this country. Perhaps most of their references were to the private sector and only some to the public sector, but certainly the secretaries believe that collective bargaining is not failing in its objective of getting management and unions to work together to reach agreements. The term that Willard Wirtz used was, once again, "the miracle of collective bargaining."

Second, it was noted that the level of employment or unemployment, particularly among young people and especially among minorities, is of great concern. Willard Wirtz spoke of the problems relating to the measurement of unemployment and the collection of such data. He discussed the need for longitudinal measures and not just periodic measures of unemployment. He also noted the interrelationship between education and manpower policy. Other secretaries discussed our "structural" employment problems but were referring to the same issues. Are training programs effective in a stable or declining region? The regional aspects of the structural employment problem were discussed by John Dunlop. Bill Usery said that we made a commitment to provide a job for everyone who is willing and able to work—that was promised by the Full Employment Act of 1946. But we have not been able to achieve that goal yet.

Third, is the point mentioned by George Shultz in his paper, which, I sense, received agreement from John Dunlop and others: the problem of the mixture of transfer payments and the proposal that a better integration of such programs is needed for low-income workers and the unemployed. George suggested that a "negative income tax" be attached to our tax system. Those things remain on the agenda.

Fourth, John Dunlop mentioned structural differences in collective bargaining. Any one who has read his book on *Industrial Relations Systems* knows how strongly he feels about overgeneralization in discussions of collective bargaining in different industries. He also believes that there needs to be more attention paid to structural change in collective-bargaining arrangements. One example is a need for structural changes in the construction industry. We all know that John has played a major role in this area, and that the secretary of labor may have to take a leadership role to achieve the needed changes in other industries.

Fifth, most of the secretaries spoke of the need for reform of the regulatory process in the Department of Labor. The central preoccupation of a large part of the department's staff is on the development of new regulations. John Dunlop described this process as "unsatisfactory," and his comments seemed to have rung a bell with the others.

Sixth, most of the secretaries seemed to agree that the management problems of the Department of Labor are important. Willard Wirtz, in particular, commented on this in his report in 1969 and again today. He discussed the need to develop management and administrative capabilities in the department. John Dunlop and William Usery also discussed this need.

CONFERENCE ON LABOR-MANAGEMENT RELATIONS,
EMPLOYMENT, AND RELATED ISSUES
ON THE OCCASION OF THE 40TH ANNIVERSARY
OF THE INDUSTRIAL RELATIONS SECTION
AND THE 25TH ANNIVERSARY OF THE
SLOAN SCHOOL OF MANAGEMENT

FRIDAY, MARCH 18, 1977

Morning Session

Little Theatre, Kresge Auditorium, MIT Campus

9:15–9:30
Welcoming Remarks and Introductions

Howard W. Johnson
Chairman, MIT Corporation

William F. Pounds
Dean, Sloan School of Management

9:30–10:30
Panel Discussion by Former Secretaries of Labor
on Labor-Management Relations and Related Issues:
Unfinished Agenda—I

Moderator: Abraham J. Siegel
Associate Dean, Sloan School of Management

Justice Arthur Goldberg

Willard Wirtz

11:00–12:25
Labor-Management Relations and Related Issues:
Unfinished Agenda—II

James D. Hodgson

John T. Dunlop

William J. Usery, Jr.

Lunch

Sala de Puerto Rico
Stratton Student Center, MIT

Introduction: Jerome B. Wiesner
President, MIT

Comments by F. Ray Marshall, Secretary of Labor
(to be read in his absence)

Afternoon Session

2:00–3:40
Panel Discussion

Moderators: Professors Charles A. Myers and Phyllis A. Wallace
Industrial Relations Section, Sloan School, MIT

Thomas R. Donahue
Executive Assistant
to the President,
AFL-CIO

William C. Mercer
President, New England
Telephone Co.

John H. Lyons
President, International
Association of Bridge and
Structural Iron Workers,
AFL-CIO

Dale D. Stone
Senior Vice President
Sun Company

Stephen I. Schlossberg
General Counsel,
United Automobile
Workers of America

Andrew C. Sigler
President, Champion
International Corporation

4:00–5:00
Open Discussion

Moderators: Professors Charles A. Myers and Phyllis A. Wallace